No One Left Behind

An unexpected educational adventure at
Machu Picchu

Debra Eckerman Pitton

Lost Lake Folk Art
SHIPWRECKT BOOKS PUBLISHING COMPANY

Minnesota

Cover photos by Deb Pitton
Cover and interior design by
Shipwreckt Books

To Father Jack Davis and Sister Peggy Byrne whose work in support of the people of Chimbote, Peru, served as the impetus for this book.

No One Left Behind

Contents

Prologue

S tanding on a small rise along the bank of the rampaging Urubamba River, I looked up at the sky. Mist clouded my vision. The raindrops grew fatter. I squinted into the haze to watch a helicopter take off, the helicopter I was supposed to be on. I'd told my students never to leave anyone behind, that if need be, they should step aside and let the next person in line board ahead of them in order to stay with another student from our Gustavus Adolphus College class. That was the rule: no one left behind. Yet there I was, left behind to watch an evacuation helicopter roar into the distance, growing smaller and smaller. My anxiety increased as the rain intensified. Standing alone on a little hill in the shadow of Machu Picchu, I realized there would be no more helicopters until the rain let up.

Twenty-one students, along with my co-teacher Mary, had just boarded a helicopter shuttling evacuees to the village of Ollantay-tambo. There they would take busses to Cusco and reunite before a short hop back to Lima; and then the eleven-hour trip home to Minnesota by way of Atlanta.

The evacuation had worked. Everyone was being carried to safety in military helicopters; everyone but me. I got left behind. I shook my head, stifled a cry, utterly alone and lost. I squeezed my eyes shut to block the tears and sat down on a rock, my head in my hands. I couldn't believe it. Over and over and over since the disastrous floods had begun, I stressed to the students, "We need to stay together." But I screwed things up when I gave my seat on the last extraction chopper to a young Canadian woman frantic at the thought of being separated from her traveling companion. My own directive had failed.

Rain collected on the back of my neck, chilling me where I sat. The smell of soggy vegetation, the roar of the river; sensory ambience surrounded me making it hard to think. I squinted upward at the rocky heights of Machu Picchu then down the raging river toward the village of Aguas Calientes. I'd have to go back there to find shelter for the night. The thought of elbowing again through the throng of young tourists, many hungry, thirsty, out of money and angry, still waiting to leave the flood ravaged town, unnerved me. The crowds had been confrontational when Mary and I left with our group of Gustavus Adolphus students; trying to push back through all those people would not be easy.

Anxiety drove the same spine-gripping tension I'd experienced so many times on this education trip to Peru. Wet, cold and close to exhaustion, I rubbed my neck and wondered, "How did I end up here on a mountain in the Andes alone?"

1. It's Meant to Be

"**I**n this world, there is poverty, and then there is misery," Father Jack Davis said in his strong baritone voice. "The people of Chimbote, Peru, live in misery."

The priest's comments intrigued me when I heard them at a fundraising dinner for Father Jack's Chimbote mission, which I attended with my friend Ruth. Ruth had traveled to Peru on a medical mission the year before and came home fired up, full of ideas to address the needs of local residents. Father Jack spoke about his parish, Our Lady of Perpetual Help, and its beautiful little church. He said the altar was an aquarium full of live fish, and that stray dogs often wandered in during services.

Father Jack's story captivated me. "Many of the people of Chimbote live in mud and straw huts with plastic sheeting for roofs, dirt floors, no indoor plumbing or electricity."

The priest talked about the soup kitchens, medical clinic and hospice he had set up in Chimbote. He described the work of the medical mission that Ruth had participated in.

"I've been working in Peru since the seventies," he said, "and we are starting to get a handle on the hunger and medical issues to some extent. What I would like to have happen next is for the children of Chimbote to learn English."

"Tourism has increased in Peru," he added. "Everyone wants to explore the Andes and visit Machu Picchu. Young people who speak English can get a job at a hotel or drive a taxi; they can raise themselves up out of extreme poverty. We've made headway in supporting basic needs. Soup kitchens help to feed the poor. The clinic provides primary healthcare. With the support of our friends here in the U.S., we also have a beautiful hospice. People can at least die with dignity. We're ready for the next step, and that is education. We've hired a few people educated well enough to serve as after school tutors to students. We try to provide the uniforms and classroom materials. Now we want to create opportunities for young people to learn to speak English so they can get jobs in tourism. But no one is available to tutor kids

1. Father Jack Davis and Sister Peggy Byrne, Mission directors.

because the local English curriculum in the schools is weak."

Ruth spoke up in a loud whisper, "Deb can do that."

I shook my head, thinking, Ruth, shut up! Don't get me into something I don't know anything about.

I wasn't an English teacher. I worked in a teacher education program at Gustavus Adolphus College. I had taken students abroad in the past, but the thought of taking students to the poor community Father Jack described sounded overwhelming.

"Teaching English is not in my skill set," I protested.

Father Jack caught my eye and headed over, greeting Ruth with a hug. Ruth introduced me. "Deb is a college professor who can totally do the English program you're talking about."

My brain was thinking fast. We had a January term course at Gustavus, which provided opportunities for educational travel and cultural experiences. I'd already taken students to Costa Rica several times to work in schools. But setting up an English language program was completely different. I had obtained a TESOL license online to support my work with students internationally. In the courses I'd taught, however, students assisted the local English teachers. Primarily, they observed in the classrooms.

"Oh no," I stammered to Father Jack when he clapped me on the back and asked me when I was coming to Peru to teach English. "I'm not qualified. The college has a lot of processes and procedures to go through before any course can be approved. I really don't think this would work. I'm not the person you want."

Father Jack had a charming smile. He put a hand on my shoulder, looked me in the eye and said, "I think Ruth is right. This is meant to be. I believe you are the one to help us make these English classes happen."

I felt a bit ashamed that I was desperately trying to avoid consideration for the task. I shook my head. Suddenly, two of my education students, Emily and Alysha, crowded beside me. Emily's father had supported the Chimbote mission, often participating himself in medical trips. He had taken the girls to Peru in January. They were attending the fundraiser just to hear Father Jack speak.

The young women shared their Peru experiences with overwhelming energy. "Deb, it would be so cool to have Gustavus education students go to Chimbote!" exclaimed Alysha. "When we were there, we helped with infants in the nursery."

"Teaching in Peru would be an awesome way for us education majors to develop our skills," Emily added. "You need to do this."

Emily's father Brian stepped over to introduce himself. "This is a great idea," he said. "I have a small foundation and would be happy to provide funding to make English classes happen in Chimbote."

Feeling pressured and still protesting, I repeated that there were lots of hoops to jump through before putting together an English program. I said again, "I really don't think I am the one to run this class. I speak very little Spanish. Organizing a full language course in Peru is not something I think I can do."

Father Jack just smiled and said, "God works in many ways. Isn't it interesting that you happened to come to this dinner with Ruth tonight? And look at the support you already have." He gestured to Alysha, Emily and Brian.

I told Father Jack that I would think about it. He said he'd be in touch, adding, "I'll pray for you as you figure out all the details."

I finished my dinner, thinking that there was no way I was going to take students to a poor and probably dangerous place. I was a former English teacher. I'd primarily taught literature, not speaking the language. I resolved not to get sucked into something I was unprepared to do. It would take a whole lot of work to put a course like Father Jack envisioned together. I wasn't sure I was capable or that I wanted to do it. I sat there, trying to come up with other reasons why I could not make these English classes happen.

The thought of starting this project made me uneasy. It wasn't that I hadn't traveled abroad, or that I didn't enjoy travel. I had visited Guatemala and Cuba as a participant in the Gustavus global faculty program. I also took students to Costa Rica, though the assignment was a fluke. My department chair was unable to go, so I filled in. My first visit to Costa Rica did not go so well. I accidentally locked myself in a bathroom and didn't have the Spanish skill to ask for help or to explain that I was locked inside. I called out feebly, unsure I would get a response. "*Hola! Yo tiene un problema*—Hello! I have a problem." I called louder and louder until someone finally came to my rescue. The family we were visiting had to take the door off the hinges to free me. I was so embarrassed. How was I supposed to know the lock didn't work? I asked my host's granddaughter how old she was, mistakenly using the word for asses instead of years. I also made the host teachers nervous when I offered to bake them *gatos*—cats, instead of *galletas*— cookies.

I don't like being in a position where I can't control the outcome. And not speaking Spanish has put me in situations I can't control. As a high school and college student, I had been able to do well by studying hard. In the classroom, teaching, I spent a lot of time preparing classes to engage my students. Running a course in a country where Spanish was needed outside the classroom, however, pushed me outside my comfort zone. My stomach tightened when I thought about all the challenges this course would pose. Establishing the course was more than I had signed on for. I decided to come up with an excuse for Father Jack, and politely decline his request.

That next Sunday in church, we sang a song that stuck in my head. I tried to ignore the connections between the song and the request from Father Jack, but the words kept haunting me. "Here I am Lord. Is it I, Lord? I have heard you calling in the night ... I will go, Lord, if you lead me. I will hold your people in my heart."

Rats, I thought. I'm feeling even more pressure, and this time from a higher power.

I was annoyed by the repetition spinning around in my head. But after a few days, ideas about a course in Peru began to slip into my mind. While I felt nervous about leading the course, I was also intrigued. Peru offered a challenge and a chance for adventure. These were things I had embraced in the past. What was making me hesitate?

My childhood and teen years were full of opportunities for adventure. Family trips, Girl Scout camping and backpacking in the wilderness were routine summer activities. I had always been eager to travel and see new places. I usually jumped at a chance to explore unknown locations or to try things I'd never done. My father had been somewhat old-school, however, and often told me that I couldn't do some things. He told me I couldn't go on a boundary waters canoe trip with my brother because I was a girl. I took that as a challenge. The more I heard "No," the more I worked to figure out a way around an obstacle and accomplish what I wanted.

This attitude worked well for me. My life was full of small successes. I enjoyed many adventures and opportunities. However, when I was in the first year of college teaching after receiving my Ph.D., I was stymied by a supervisor who disagreed with my philosophy of teaching. She gave me negative reviews, and ultimately fired me.

I was shocked. My goal had been to teach at a college. Facing such a setback rocked my self-confidence and I slipped into depression. Working with great health care professionals, I climbed out of the dark pit and returned to work and family life, but I was left with the fear of failure hidden behind an even stronger need to control situations in order to ensure success.

Fear of failing weighed on me. Folks who set up my earlier international courses knew the language and supported me during my time abroad. If I went to Peru, I would be on my own, and that felt scary.

I'd have to visit the host country before taking students there. The Center for International Culture and Education, CICE, only had limited funds, and the small amount they provided for the site visit would not get me everywhere I needed to go. Since I didn't have the money to personally fund a trip to Peru, I relaxed, believing the project would never get off the ground. "Oh well," I thought to myself, "I'm off the hook. I tried."

What I didn't know was that Emily had been badgering her father to help get the course rolling. Her father, Brian, contacted me to ask where I was in the process. I told him that I wasn't able to propose a course because I hadn't visited the country and explained that I didn't have enough money to spend a week to ten days vetting the location.

Brian said that he would help fund my site visit.

I shot back a message saying that I would also need a translator due to my lack of Spanish proficiency. This, I thought, would certainly be the end of things. I received another message from Brian. "I'll pay for someone to go with you," he said. Suddenly

2. Mission of Our Lady of Perpetual Help in Chimbote.

cornered in spite of my efforts to avoid teaching the Peru course, I ran out of excuses.

Ruth suggested that I take my daughter Laura to translate. The idea appealed to me. Laura traveled to Costa Rica with me when she was twelve and she fell in love with the culture and the language. As a result, she continued Spanish classes and eventually chose to major in it at college. She jumped at the chance to go to Peru, eagerly offering to sign on as my traveling companion and translator. Taking directions from my daughter would be a switch.

Still, my weak Spanish skills left me hesitant to seize the Peru opportunity. Laura said I had enabled myself not to learn Spanish by always traveling with translation support, which was true. I had taken Spanish classes but never seem to retain what I learned in class. The language mental block was frustrating. I understood more Spanish than I could speak, but I was hesitant to use the language. I made sure I had language support when I traveled, primarily because I didn't want to make any mistakes.

"*Yo tengo poquito Español.*—I have very little Spanish," I repeated, adding that I was, "*una maestra de English.*—an English teacher." This always got me off the hook.

The discomfort I felt speaking Spanish on that first trip to Costa Rica was offset by the support I received there. The schools felt familiar. We followed a structure. And translators spoke Spanish for me. I took students to Costa Rica on multiple occasions and things always went well. No miscommunication.

I prided myself on being flexible and open to new ideas and experiences. Still, the lack of existing structure and support in Peru bothered me. I would need to work out all the details and find ways for students to teach with limited resources. In addition, I'd be responsible for keeping everyone safe while living in a very poor area. The task felt overwhelming. If I accepted Father Jack's invitation, I would have to convince myself first that I could conquer my fears and enjoy the challenge.

My thoughts went back and forth over the pros and cons of traveling to Peru. Eventually, the plus side won out. Considering the possibilities, I decided on a service-learning course open to all students, not just education majors. English instruction would be our primary focus, however, engagement, the interaction with residents of Chimbote, might end up being the best part of the Peru course.

Still a bit unsure I could pull it off, imagining the course started to excite me. The opportunity for adventure called, trumping my initial fear. Peru. Machu Picchu. What was there to worry about?

2. Making it Happen

F unding from Gustavus Adolphus, combined with a generous contribution from Brian, Emily's father, allowed me to schedule a site visit in January 2009. I went determined to learn enough about the location to set up the course. When Laura and I landed in Peru, a man in the airport lobby held a sign with our names on it. I asked him his name. He replied, "Hector Cortez."

I'd been given a different name of the person who would meet us. Immediately, my stomach clenched. A typical nervous reaction.

"We were expecting someone else," I explained.

Hector shrugged and said in his clear but strongly accented English, "Then you will be waiting here a long time because the person from the mission could not come. I am here to meet you and set up your visit."

When I asked why I hadn't been informed of the change, Hector shrugged again. Laura gave me a nudge and said that the change seemed reasonable. Still, I was uncomfortable and hesitated in the swirl of people heading in and out of the airport. Laura gave me another little shove and said, "Let's go."

I thought about all the ways leaving with a stranger could go wrong but nodded and followed Hector to his car. He was about my age, tall and serious, with dark eyes and wavy hair.

To my great relief, Hector talked about Father Jack and the mission. "My travel company provides support for volunteers working at the mission in Chimbote."

Hector set us up in a hotel then outlined a detailed plan for our travels. It was important to check out as many places as possible, besides the mission, for students to visit. To accomplish this, Hector created a very full itinerary. His list of directions made the student trip sound overwhelming. I took copious notes and tried to keep details straight. When we finished, Hector started to leave.

I looked at Laura. "Is there anything else we should ask?"

An eager nineteen-year-old, my daughter just smiled. With no further questions from us, Hector left. His site visit directions seemed complicated yet somewhat vague. I worried we'd end up getting lost in Chimbote.

The next day, things started out well enough with a bus trip from Lima to Chimbote, though six hours looking at the desert and the coastline got tiring. We were given lunch, which was nothing I'd ever seen or eaten before. There were videos to watch, and a bingo game run by the bus hostess. Everyone spoke in rapid Spanish, so even Laura struggled a bit to follow what was said. I was never completely sure we were on the right bus.

When we finally stopped at a bus station, I was hesitant to leave the bus. There was no sign announcing the name of the town. Neither Laura nor I understood what the hostess had said. We stepped down from the bus and wandered around a dusty parking lot. No one came to meet us, so I immediately began to feel my heart rate accelerate, and my stomach tightened.

I was ready to get back on the bus and try to return to Lima but that could mean we'd end up somewhere else totally unknown. I spied an old pay phone, pulled out the number for the mission and made a call. An operator answered. I wasn't sure if she was asking for the number I was calling or telling me how many coins I needed to insert. Laura grabbed the phone out of my hand and asked a few questions. Just then, I heard someone call my name. A smiling young woman walked up and introduced herself as the Volunteer Coordinator. I felt a rush of relief. She'd come to take us to the mission.

My relief quickly changed to anxiety again after we got into the van and began bouncing over the rough road at high speed. We swerved and dodged around the other cars, and at one point drove up on the sidewalk to pass a vehicle. For some reason, our driver was in a huge rush to get us to the mission. I made a mental note to set up taxi service for the students when we arrived, hoping to avoid crazy van rides.

We pulled up in front of the mission and jerked to a stop. Laura and I discovered a cool oasis inside the complex that was very different from the heat and dust stirred up by the van. Our Lady of Perpetual Help mission was just as my friend Ruth had described it, white stone and palm trees, a roof of woven fronds. Calm and peaceful.

We dumped our bags in the dorm and wandered around until we unexpectedly ran into a small group of college students visiting the mission for the week from Saint John's and Saint Benedict, two schools also located in Minnesota. They invited us to join them in their routine.

The Johnnies and Bennies stayed in local homes and did whatever Father Jack asked them to do. They escorted kids to the local pool for a swim and helped to repair old wheelchairs.

Father Jack had built dorms for visitors to the mission, and the Gustavus International Committee recommended that my group stay in them feeling that dorms would be safer than living in the community. Laura was disappointed we didn't stay with a Peruvian family, but I was personally glad to stay at the mission where I could speak English. The limited English I heard spoken by local residents meant that almost all students would teach basic English.

The mission housed a small library and had several classrooms with desks and chalkboards. Although the classrooms were very basic, they would work for what I had in mind. The number of desks would determine how many local children we could accommodate. I made a note to bring teaching materials with us to ensure that we had what we needed to engage our Chimbote students.

The dorm Laura and I stayed in was simple and clean. Each dorm room had one bathroom with a shower. The showers often produced only cold water. Wooden twin beds lined the walls, with a nightstand and light next to each bed.

Father Jack said he could manage about twenty students. Keeping track of that many college students seemed daunting, but I understood the importance of putting several student teachers in each classroom, so twenty students it would be.

There was no air conditioning and no fans. It would be hot. In fact, the heat alone would be a challenging environment for Minnesota college students.

The Johnnies and the Bennies constructed a simple bed as a part of their service, and we accompanied them to deliver it to a home that had just one sleeping area for an entire family. The home consisted of walls woven from reeds, dirt floors, a cook stove and an outhouse. Although we were helping, stepping into such poverty felt voyeuristic. I wondered if it was ok to even be there, or was it cruel? Home visits opened the hearts and minds of college students who had had no earlier concept of poverty. But were home visits necessary? In order to understand the struggle to survive faced by many Peruvians every day, maybe we needed to feel uncomfortable.

I confess, touring communities around the mission, I wrinkled my nose more than once and looked to see Laura's reaction. Dirt roads, dust and strange odors were challenging. The heat. Constantly sweating. I questioned whether this was a good climate for a long visit. The college students I knew were accustomed to relatively clean Minnesota air and grassy spaces between classroom buildings, and I worried they might not cope well. Laura, on the other hand, gave me confidence that the students would quickly adapt. She seemed not to mind anything. I hoped her reaction would be typical of Gustavus students.

The mission staff were very gracious. When Laura and I helped serve a soup meal after Sunday Mass, many who'd come to eat murmured "Thanks." With little Spanish, I smiled and made few comments. Laura, just starting work on a Spanish degree, chatted easily with people. Her interactions revealed a glimmer of the potential relationships my students might develop.

Exploring the community, however, I wondered if Father Jack's plan to provide English classes was really what the people of Chimbote wanted, or even needed. I had mixed feelings.

3. Street scene near the mission.

Gustavus faculty and students, a significant majority of whom are white, come from relative privilege. I definitely didn't want to lead a group that wanted to ride into Peru to save the poor. Service-learning courses were designed to respond to local needs. I asked to set up a focus group of local adults and young people to discuss their reactions to the proposed English classes.

With Laura as my translator, I organized a group of people to come to the mission and share their thoughts. We provided ice cream as an incentive to encourage people to talk. Getting the ice cream from a *tienda*—a local home store and keeping it in the kitchen freezer seemed like a good plan, but it didn't work out so well during our conversation. Before we got through even one question, people were spooning up pools of melted ice cream.

I wanted to know what English skills the children learned in the local schools hoping to assess whether there was a need for English classes. Would parents actually bring their children to the mission for English classes if we offered them?

Their passionate responses overwhelmed me. Even without Laura's translation, I could tell that this was something people were excited about. They said it would be a positive experience for the local youth.

"We need our children to have English so they can drive a taxi or work with tourists," was one reply. Another pointed out that while English was taught in local schools, the teachers used rote memorization and concentrated only on written English. The group made it clear that they wanted their children to learn to speak English so that they could talk to visitors and volunteers who came to Chimbote. They believed English would secure future jobs.

"We see a good life for our children if they can talk English and help out visitors," someone stated. The focus group participants assured me that there would be many children attending the program in January during the regular school break.

I reviewed my notes and began to consider how I could set up the classes. I wanted all education majors to be comfortable teaching English, even if they knew no Spanish, similar to an English Language Learner classroom in the States. It would be a great experience for my students and the youth who would benefit. Obviously, the local children wouldn't learn a lot of English in a couple of weeks, however, we could help them acquire English terms and phrases. Ideally, the short program would create interest and enthusiasm for continuing English language studies.

In addition to checking out the teaching curriculum, I wanted to know how to keep my college students entertained while they were at the mission. Some college students are prone to partying. This I knew. Perhaps those who signed up for the course were not the party animal type. In any case, I looked for opportunities for them to safely explore the community and the country.

At the end of our stay, the Johnnie and Bennie students invited Laura and me to join them on a scheduled trip up a nearby mountain, one with a huge cross at the top. That seemed like a good idea, so we piled into a small van and started up the hillside. The winding road with sheer drop-offs on either side scared the crap out of me. Laura laughed and screamed with the other college students. The van had to stop, pull up to the edge of a cliff, then back up in order to get around several steep curves. It was nerve wracking. I was panicky, and practically climbed over the back of my seat to get away from what appeared to be eminent death when it looked like we were driving over the edge of a cliff. And of course, there were no seatbelts in the van.

When we finally arrived at the top, my stomach was so queasy from the drive, I thought I was going to be sick.

The students felt otherwise. "Awesome," "What a rush," and "That was so cool."

After a few deep breaths to calm myself, I caught up with the others who'd run over to explore a symbolic underground opening into the chapel site. We entered, ducked our heads to avoid hitting the ceiling and shuffled through a dark tunnel so narrow that our shoulders brushed the walls and so dark we couldn't see our hands in front of our faces.

Next thing I know, we stumbled out into full sunlight facing a statue of Christ hanging above us in an open-air chapel. The students took in that scene then scrambled to the top of the mountain where a huge cross stood out against the bright blue sky. When I tried to climb a few yards up rock piles toward the summit, a wave of dizziness forced me to sit down. I shook my head at the students making their way up the mountain, their figures growing smaller.

Laura was gracious enough to stay with me. "What do you think about the experience so far? Do you think college students like yourself will be ok working here, and doing stuff like climbing this mountain?"

"Sure," Laura replied. "It's really cool."

Myself, I still worried that taking on this course might push me past my comfort level. I liked a good adventure as much as anybody, but all the unknowns scared me.

What if one of the students gets hurt?

What if one of them falls climbing this mountain?

Drive up the mountain in that shaky van? That was not safe!

What about evenings? Would the students be safe at night?

They would absolutely have to drink bottled water.

What if someone forgot and got sick? What if someone got really, really sick?

Shaken by the sudden onslaught of my concerns and misgivings, I decided to walk down the mountain. I didn't want to risk another van ride down the treacherous switchback road. The students I bring would probably want to make the trip up the mountain to see

4. Chimbote from the mountain.

the cross, but they could hike up and avoid the dangerous ride in the van. I would see to that. Maybe.

I insisted that Laura accompany me on my hike down. After only a few turns in the dust and the heat down the narrow road, she stopped. The van had been slowly following us, the driver waving to us to get in.

Laura decided she wasn't walking any farther. "It's too hot and too far," she said. "Really, Mom, do you think Father Jack would let us come up here if he didn't know the drivers were safe?"

Being chastised by my daughter was uncomfortable to say the least, but I was dirty and sweaty. I paused a second to look down the long mountain road, then clambered inside the bus.

"I'm only riding down to get out of the sun," I said to Laura.

"Sure," she commented sarcastically.

Over the next few days, Laura and I soldiered on, helping out at the mission. All too soon, it was time to leave. After a gracious thank you and send-off from Father Jack and his parishioners, Laura and I headed back to Lima and got ready to travel to Machu Picchu and other ancient Peruvian sites.

A similar trip to Machu Picchu at the end of classes in Chimbote would serve as great motivation for the Gustavus students. I figured that I could keep everyone on task during two weeks of teaching. We could take a trip to the mountain and the beach for relaxation on the weekends. Lots of lesson planning and games would take up our evenings. We'd go out into the community for a group dinner at a local restaurant once each week. Machu Picchu would be a key piece of the experience.

As I continued to plan what this course would look like, I began to see that it could be a powerful learning opportunity for students. Teaching in Peru, developing empathy for people with an entirely different culture, language, lifestyle and economic system would carry far into their teaching future. Thinking about the discussions we might have at night, revisiting daily experiences, excited me.

The long bus ride back to the capitol proved relaxing because I was more at ease. I ate the food and I had no qualms about trying whatever was served. Gazing out at the shifting dunes and distant ocean, I marveled at the sameness of the countryside that went on for miles. The trip to Chimbote had gone well. The site visit provided me with enough information to feel comfortable about managing whatever might come up during the teaching portion of our course time in Peru.

Hector met us again in Lima. He mapped out the rest of our itinerary, which included a bus ride through the Sacred Valley of the Incas, with stops at several ancient sites. Hector seemed a lot friendlier as he ran through the complex steps of the next part of our journey. Maybe I was just more comfortable around him. He told us that after traveling by bus the first day, we would switch to a taxi on day two. After lunch, we would visit more archeological sites and spend the second night at a small hotel. In the morning, we'd take another taxi to the train station. From there, we would head to Aguas Calientes and the famous Inca site of Machu Picchu. The schedule intrigued me, in spite of all the details I would have to remember.

Unfortunately, things didn't go as planned. We flew into Cusco, where the higher altitude brought on altitude sickness almost immediately. Laura was fine. The illness, caused by the thin air at high altitudes, produces headaches and nausea. I drank a lot of the coca tea provide by the hotel. The tea was an ancient Incan remedy derived from the same plant as cocaine. I made it through the first day thanks to the tea, multiple doses of Tylenol, and wearing my sunglasses, even indoors, to soften the piercing sunlight. Still, I felt nauseous and had a monster headache. I couldn't sleep. The food tasted awful. But, in order to plan for where my college students could go, I was determined to complete the site visit to Machu Picchu.

Following several stops at Inca sites and a native lunch, we left the bus tour. A taxi picked us up and drove us to a quaint hotel for the night. All of the transportation switches struck me as a little dicey, but Laura remained my canary in the mineshaft. If she said a situation was ok, I pushed away my apprehension.

The next day, we managed things just fine. Laura continued to be the point person, describing the sights to me, sharing her thoughts as we drove through the Scared Valley. The bright sun only made my headache worse. I kept my eyes closed as much as possible.

We were supposed to meet our taxi driver early the following morning for the ride to the train station. We didn't want to miss our departure, so we had asked the driver to pick us up at the hotel at six a.m. sharp. Upon arriving at the station in Ollantaytambo, the driver held his hand out for payment. I tried to explain that Hector had arranged for all costs to be included in our trip fee. Hector said we didn't need to pay anything, not even a tip. The driver shook his head, his hand out.

"Laura, tell him everything's been paid for. I'm not spending more when we don't need to," I said.

Laura tried to explain, but the taximan shook his head again and kept his hand out. We went back and forth for a while in a sort of sign language. The driver held his hand out, palm up. I showed him our itinerary with "payment in full" stamped on it. Finally, Laura realized that the driver was not the same driver we had the previous day. He'd been waiting outside the hotel for any rider to get in. His vehicle was not our designated taxi.

I paid the fee and we headed over to the station. I still felt awful. And now I was irritated. I had clearly messed up. I'd have to make it through another day using Tylenol, and that morning, my thinking was fuzzy. The headache worsened. I felt like I had glass shards stuck in my eyes. The pain was intense.

When we arrived in Aguas Calientes for the van ride up to Machu Picchu, my altitude sickness blossomed. The ancient city, however, was actually lower in altitude than Cusco. My headache eased somewhat as the morning wore on. We managed to find the right bus for the ride up the mountain to meet with our English-speaking guide.

Headache or not, Machu Picchu was amazing. The first view of this ancient Inca site completely stunned me. This leg of the trip would be an important part of the course. How could students not be impressed by a civilization that built such impressive structures without the help of modern machinery?

The sunlight and altitude remained challenging. I moved hesitantly on a narrow path winding along sheer drop-offs into the river gorge far below. At one point, Laura stopped and took my hand to lead me along.

"Honestly," she said as we inched forward, "You're stumbling around so much, I think you're going to fall off the cliff."

I appreciated her help more than I could say. The hotel had given us coca tea that morning, which was also reputed to provide an energy boost. But I felt sluggish, and I battled a headache that wouldn't quit. I wondered, what would I do if I were incapacitated like this when I returned with students? What if my students were affected by the altitude like I was?

Laura was unfazed by the elevation, so I hoped that perhaps it was my age that made me susceptible to altitude sickness. I vowed to find something to help mitigate the effects. Surely there was something that would enable me to function in the mountains.

After Machu Picchu, we returned to Cusco by train to complete scheduled visits to several other important and interesting Inca sites in the area. At one stop, a woman with a llama offered to pose with folks from our bus. Laura, excited for a llama photo, moved in close to the animal only to receive a slobbery lick from a huge llama tongue. She laughed and exclaimed that I should arrange for all future students to be kissed by a llama.

That night I called Hector to explain our taxi mix up. He was not happy that I had messed up his careful plan for us. Not being able to understand the language made me feel inadequate and somewhat stupid. How could I be in charge of a group when I made mistakes like the one with the taxi? My head was still pounding. Thinking straight was difficult.

I had to admit that I really preferred to be the person in charge, the one who knew what was going on. Being under the control of my nineteen-year-old daughter was uncomfortable to say the least. Nothing we encountered bothered Laura. She was eager to explore every site. My dependence on Laura, and her enthusiasm for everything, led me to think that learning to rely on someone else would be a benefit for my student teachers. Perhaps traveling to a country where they didn't know the language, where they needed to depend on others who were not like them, might shift their perspective in a positive way.

When we finally got back to Lima and my head cleared, we met with Hector again to review the student trip to Peru in January. We discussed which locations to keep and which ones to skip. Wanting a college student's perspective, I asked Laura.

"The bus trip and all the stops in the Sacred Valley were interesting, but there were way too many ruins. Seeing all the other sites first kind of diminished the impact of Machu Picchu," she replied. "I suggest you take the train directly to Machu Picchu and only visit the Inca sites close to Cusco."

Hector explained there were medications available to combat the symptoms of altitude sickness. "The medication will enable you and your students to adjust more easily to the altitude." He also informed me that most hotels in Cusco and Aguas Calientes provided oxygen for travelers in need of it. I wondered why I hadn't been told that earlier.

We made a tentative plan for the actual course. I told Hector I would be in touch to finalize it. I still had reservations.

Would students respond positively to teaching at the mission in Chimbote? Would I have time to get the students ready to be effective in a classroom full of non-English speaking kids? Would they find the living conditions too difficult, too different from what they were used to? And what if they got sick or hurt in Cusco or Machu Picchu? There wasn't a medical facility nearby.

Considering these issues, how could I ensure the course would be successful?

I thought about an experience from one of my earlier trips to Costa Rica. A student had exhibited signs of what seemed to be appendicitis. I managed to get her to a hospital and finally home safely without any problems. I reminded myself that I had handled a potential medical emergency in a foreign country, and it had turned out ok. Still, I had this kernel of doubt rolling around my brain. Costa Rica had a modern hospital where we were able to check out the student's symptoms. In the mountains headed to Machu Picchu, what facility would be available?

Back at the airport, ready to head home, I asked Laura if she thought the course, with the work at the mission, the conditions in Chimbote, and the possibility of altitude sickness, might be too much.

"Maybe I shouldn't offer the course. Maybe students won't be interested."

Laura rolled her eyes at me. "Oh Mom," she said, "don't be so nervous about everything. Think about how great this course will be for your students. I learned a bunch of stuff, and they will, too. I mean, what college kid wouldn't want to go on an adventure like this?"

3. Education, Healthcare, and Poverty in Peru: Week One

 week before my co-teacher Mary and I arrived in Chimbote escorting twenty-one college students, the mission distributed fliers around town to announce, "Free English classes! All children come in the morning; all adults come in the afternoon." Father Jack had been recruiting for the classes at Sunday Mass as well, and said he thought we would have about seventy-five students.

I called the course, "Education, Healthcare, and Poverty in Peru: A Service-learning Experience." Fifteen Gustavus Adolphus undergrads would teach English and six would work in healthcare.

When I returned from the site visit, I laid out the work students would do at the mission and the health clinic, as well as a schedule for classes. Even after describing the success of the site visit, however, I got pushback from the approval committee. They questioned how I would keep the students safe and asked how I would prepare them for the difficult environment.

I replied to the committee that all students would read and discuss the *Peru Reader* to prepare for our journey. I assured the committee that the mission was safe—that we would have local guards when we left the mission walls, parish men hired by Father Jack. They monitored the gate and accompanied all volunteers when they left the complex. Father Jack had stated adamantly that he was committed to providing a safe environment for anyone who came to his mission. I'd told the committee I was planning group excursions to prevent students from going out on their own and to keep them all so busy teaching classes and planning lessons that they would be too exhausted at night to think about other activities. Although I responded with this additional information, the committee denied approval for the course.

While I might have cheered this news earlier, after my site visit, I knew going to Peru was an experience that could change the lives of participating students. I appealed the committee's decision and met with the members personally to argue that we needed to expose our students to challenges in the world, to enable them to experience and empathize with people from other countries and cultures. One faculty member said that the litigious nature of the U.S., and some of our students' parents, made international study a risky venture.

"There is just as much danger involved in spending a night drinking in Minneapolis," I responded, "and we don't monitor students' weekend social lives."

The committee's reaction really sealed the deal for me. I did not like to be told "No," especially when I'd developed solid reasons for offering the course. All of my hesitation, nervousness and fear melted away in response to being denied their approval.

I sent a letter to each committee member. I outlined my argument, included research on service learning and restated my belief that the Peru experience would help students develop a more realistic perspective of the world as well as the needs of others.

My arguments worked, the committee reconsidered, and we were headed for Peru.

We flew into Lima late at night. Hector met us in the airport. We followed him like a line of ducks through the building and across the parking lot to our bus. Students took in the rush of Spanish that surrounded us. They inhaled the ocean breeze and strained to see the palm trees. It was dark and we had an early morning pick-up to go to the bus station, so we didn't see much of the Peruvian Capital.

When we arrived at the Hostal Gémina, we wearily hauled our suitcases up to our rooms. We were on the second and third floors, and there was only a tiny elevator. After a short night's sleep, we hastily grabbed the breakfast rolls and gulped coffee. We arrived at the bus station with little time to spare. Hector helped us get luggage on board and take our seats. He had gotten us tickets to the upper level of the bus, where we could see clearly out the large windows as we headed out of Lima.

The students each experienced the six-hour bus ride to Chimbote very differently. Some were leery of the food service, some were awestruck by the stretch of unending desert, many were nervous about the curvy road and steep drop offs along the ocean.

Looking at the dilapidated shacks stacked up on top of each other along the sandy hillsides as we left Lima, Kyle J turned to me and said, "What have you gotten me into, Deb?!" I just smiled back in response.

The students took a lot of pictures, engaged in lively conversations and played card games. The ride helped them get to know each other better. When we finally disembarked the air-conditioned bus in Chimbote, we all blinked in the strong sunlight and wilted a bit in the heat. Alison, always on top of things, found Julio's passport after it had fallen out of his pocket and onto the bus floor. She walked over to him, waved the passport to tease him, then handed over the little blue book. "How do you think you will get home without this?" she asked.

I was beginning to understand the difficulty of keeping the students safe and avoiding problems like lost passports. What a mess it would have been if Alison hadn't spotted Julio's passport before we got off the bus! I gave him a stern look, but he just grinned sheepishly, his dark eyes twinkling, and said, "Thanks, Alison. I might get left behind if I don't have this."

Father Jack sent the new mission volunteer coordinator, Charles, to meet us with a mission van and a truck. No taxis. Students gazed worriedly as drivers hastily piled their luggage onto the back of the truck, creating a mountain that the drivers secured with a bit of rope.

We piled into the van and started off for the mission. A donkey pulling a rickshaw-like vehicle full of corn stalks moved slowly down the dusty road. Students dangled out of the windows, taking in the sights. I cringed when the van driver passed another car by going up on the sidewalk and around a light pole. I remembered that driving in Chimbote did not include using seat belts. Our journey seemed to be a kind of race to see who could get wherever they were going the fastest. When Mary turned to look at me apprehensively, I just shrugged. We were in Peru; we were committed to the experience, no matter what. Roaring down dusty streets, we managed to arrive at the mission without losing any bags or students.

We settled into the dorms and began to adjust to our new home. Father Jack gave us a tour of the community and told the story of how he came to be in Chimbote. There'd been an earthquake in the

70s that devastated the city and he came to help. And he stayed.

"The local people were mostly fishermen. They'd been able to provide for their families until big fishing companies began fishing the waters. The small boats could not keep up," he explained.

The fish cannery, while providing some jobs, polluted the water close to the town, and emitted odors that were at times overwhelming to local residents. Chimbote's unemployment rate was high, and Father Jack, having been a visiting priest for several years, felt a calling to work with the people. He was eventually released from his duties in the States to serve the mission permanently.

5. Teacher and student in Chimbote.

With his charismatic appeal, Father Jack created a network of donors and sponsors who provided funds to support community needs. He told us about hiding from members of the communist party of Peru, Shining Path, during their uprising in the 1980s when his life was threatened. He explained that he and Sister Peggy, a former teacher who joined him to provide tutoring and educational support, had worked in Chimbote for many years. Originally from the Fargo, North Dakota area, it was easy to see how Father Jack, with his positive assertiveness, and Sister Peggy, with her sweet Irish accent and quiet determination, were able to raise funds to support the mission.

Because the Gustavus students weren't all education majors, I'd appointed team leaders for planning each of the classes. I also divided our teachers, depending on their own interest and experience, into groups to work with different age students. We planned to hold morning classes for ages 5-6, 7-8, 9-10 and 11-12. In the afternoon, we would hold classes for ages 13-14, 15-16, 17-18. Adult classes were held in the evening. Our structure resulted in four classrooms with three teachers in each group.

Health care students would be out in the community all day, helping at the small clinic and the hospice. We planned to reconnect in the evenings. I felt ready and eager for us to get going.

Sunday morning, I assigned classrooms for the teachers and

6. Gustavus healthcare student providing in-home care.

worked with them to set up a seating arrangement that would provide space for activities. Then we toured local neighborhoods to get a sense of the community. As we walked around, the students were especially struck by the lovely hospice Father Jack had created, as well as the small, functional clinic.

I made sure to give health care students directions to share with taxis they would have to take to the hospice and clinic. I worried a bit about them traveling on their own, but Mary would coordinate this process. I hoped they'd get around ok.

Sarah B., Nicole, Laura and the other nursing students were all very serious about their work. They brought scrubs to wear as well as gloves and surgical masks, just in case—something I hadn't thought of doing.

A few little glitches surfaced as we got started. For instance, when we unpacked supplies sent in a container, I noticed that a lot of books and supplies were missing. Sister Peggy explained that she had used some of the resources for an optional after-school tutoring program for local youth. It was great that the materials were helpful, but it left us a little short of supplies. I was glad I had brought some paper and markers and stuff with me.

Another problem cropped up because Kyle G. had traveled with a severe rash, a reaction to strep throat medication he'd been taking before we left. He was pretty miserable, so Charles took him to the clinic to get some cream to relieve the itching. When Kyle showed up back in the mission a half hour later, he said he had been given a shot.

"What?" I asked. "They gave you a shot? What kind? Was it sterile?"

My concern about the sanitary conditions at the clinic was obvious.

"I think it was just cortisone," responded Kyle G. Tall and lanky, a laid-back kid, he hadn't complained much about the rash, even though it looked awful. "I already feel better," he said.

"Ok, well, let's not tell the folks back in Minnesota that you got a shot, and we aren't sure what it was," I answered.

Kyle G. smiled and said, "No worries."

And that was that.

7. Piggyback ride in Chimbote.

Monday morning at nine, the health care students donned their scrubs and headed to their assigned sites, and the teachers prepared to greet their first students. We watched children pour through the mission gates accompanied by their mothers or older siblings. I looked around and thought to myself, "We are going to need a bigger space!"

More than one hundred twenty-five kids showed up. We thought we would have around seventy-five. We had to do some scrambling and some quick rearranging to fit everyone into the rooms.

Each group made name tags and started with introductions and *me gusta*—what they liked. After a slow, shy beginning, it became clear that the children were eager to participate. It was ovbious that oral English was not something they did in school. But they were excited to learn.

We discussed the enthusiasm and energy of the morning classes at lunch and students began to plan for ways to break the larger classes into smaller groups for better interaction. The students admitted they were tired after this first class and were happy to take part in the Peruvian custom of siesta. The one-hour rest after lunch provided a much-needed nap for many, and relaxation and conversation time for the others. I had never been one to take a nap, but after lying on my cot, I dozed off. I was glad I had a travel alarm clock so I could roust out the students to prepare for their next classes.

That first afternoon, we had around fifty older teens, ages fourteen to twenty. Twenty-five adults showed up for our night classes. These numbers were a little more manageable, and the college students re-laxed.

The heath care team came back with stories about the lack of supplies in the clinic. They'd helped roll gauze for bandages that were used in lieu of ready-made items. They were eager for the next day when they would accompany local nurses to homes to help with the pa-tients unable to make it to the clinic.

8. More than 125 students showed up on the first morning of classes.

The second morning, almost seventy-five additional children showed up. I felt we were full to capacity and tried to turn away the new students, but they cried, *"Por Favor. Inglis."* And so, we squeezed them in until were over-full. In some of the rooms we squeezed two kids into each seat, and still we had Peruvian children sitting on the floor.

When we were packed in with no more space available, I did have to turn some kids away. I felt awful, but I didn't want to overwhelm my students, many who had never taught before. We had rooms with more than fifty children crammed in. With the help of my Spanish speakers, I posted a sign on the mission gate: *"Las clases de Inglés están cerradas,"* to let people know the classes were closed. Still, the *Mamás* pleaded with me to let their children join the English classes. Julio, a native Spanish speaker and most fluent in our group, told me he could not turn away the children.

"When the mothers ask, '*Por favor, ¿puedo inscribir a mi hijo en las clases de inglés?* —Please, can I enroll my child in the English classes?' I can't refuse." Julio managed to sneak even more children into his classroom when I wasn't looking.

I spent the first week roaming from class to class, helping out, providing resources and ideas as needed. We all appreciated the meals and the hour-long siesta that followed lunch each day. Classes ran from 9:00-11:30 a.m., and from 2:00-4:30 p.m. We took chaperoned walks to the local store at the end of classes for Peruvian candy, ice cream and Inca Cola, which tasted like bubble gum. The students always seemed to be hungry.

The food at the mission was simple, but good. We had lots of local dishes, including *Cuy*—guinea pig, and *Ceviche*—raw fish prepared in citric lime juice. Both were native dishes. We especially enjoyed fresh mangos and avocados. Mujura, our cook and a Chimbote native, also prepared chicken and pasta to balance local food with more common American dishes. When meals were served, the college students devoured almost everything.

In the early evenings, after dinner, the Gustavus students played volleyball and soccer in the dirt field next to the mission. We often got a loud game of Charades or Celebrity going afterward in the "Gringo room," the name for the common space available for volunteers. We planned for the next day's classes, with students making paper notebooks and drawings to help teach the language. I was proud of their hard work, and appreciative of the education majors taking the lead with ideas and activities for their groups, as well as the willingness of the rest of the team to jump in with the teaching.

We held reflection sessions at night to discuss student experiences, managing their emotions and reactions. Mary and I took the students to the rooftop patio, candle-lit to create a more thoughtful mood, and asked them how they felt mentally and physically.

Mary made the rounds with the health care team, visiting sick people, many of them suffering from one form of cancer or another. The students were horrified. They said that cancer was awful enough when a person had access to treatment, but when no treatment existed, it was tragic. The health care students felt the futility of the visits to such patients and shared their feelings during our reflection sessions. Jeanifer, a nursing student who had witnessed a patient wasting away due to lack of medicine that was readily available in the States, was the most vocal regarding the inequity and unfairness facing Chimbote residents living in poverty.

The students who were teaching also felt overwhelmed. Providing English lessons and keeping the children engaged was difficult. The crowded classrooms were hot, and the young students were often loud and rambunctious. Our youngest group of Chimbotano students, we realized, had not been in a school setting before. The teachers had to deal with separation anxiety and tears as mothers peeled their little children's

9. Chimbote students with a Gustavus English teacher.

fingers off their legs at the start of class. Molly and her team handled it well, providing hugs to the little ones who needed extra support. We realized that the attention span of these youngsters was short. The teachers had their hands full trying to keep the kids involved so they could learn a few words of English.

At the reflection sessions, my students also discussed whether they were really providing much impact. Considering that we had to start with the basics, and we had such a short time with the students, there was not much depth to the English lessons.

"I can't figure out what to do about my feelings," Julio said. "I know we're providing something for these kids, but seeing such poverty, I just don't know how to feel. I can't put it into words."

His thoughts were echoed by most of the rest of the students. They felt sad, they felt like they wanted to do more, yet they also noted how fun and gracious the students were, thanking them at the end of each class. Mary was great at leading these discussions. She pointed out that we were showing the children and adults in our classes, and the patients at the clinic and hospice, that they were valued. As hard as it was to see kids coming to class in the same clothing every day, playing with junk in the street, we were showing that they were not forgotten, letting them know that there were people who cared about them.

Father Jack and Sister Peggy were great cheerleaders for all of us, greeting us in the mornings, observing and joining in the outdoor games of 'Hokey Pokey' and 'Simon Says.' At the end of the first week, we took Jack, Peggy and the Gustavus students to a very nice restaurant in Nuevo Chimbote. We stopped on the way at a Catholic cathedral that had recently been built. Father Jack asked the students to think about this church and contrast it with the mission chapel. The opulence and beauty of the cathedral and the paved streets of Nuevo Chimbote were far different from the dusty streets and simple hand painted images in the mission.

The restaurant, a steak house recommended by Charles, was a great place to unwind. The students, whom I'd cautioned not to drink or even purchase alcohol during the week, in accordance with mission regulations, avoided the local Inca Cola as a beverage option and celebrated the completion of their first week of teaching with Coca-Cola. Joking and boisterous conversations turned quiet as the dinner wound down. The college students looked at the leftovers still on the table. "Let's take this food back to the guys who work at the gate and walk us to the *tienda*," someone suggested.

So, we loaded up meals in to-go boxes and took back the French fries and chunks of steak we could not finish. When I was sitting in the patio after we got back, Julio, Brandon and Kyle J. came up to me.

"That was pretty sneaky, having us pig out at that restaurant," they said.

"What do you mean? "I inquired.

"We enjoyed it, but we feel bad about eating so much when everyone here probably has never had a meal like that."

Although I had not intended it to happen, the students felt guilty about splurging at the restaurant. When we met for our next reflection, several said the experience made them stop and think about how many people go hungry each day. "I see the little kids in my class looking so thin and I wonder how much they get to eat," Molly said. Although a secondary education major, I had put her in with the youngest students, the five-year-olds, because she had always shown such great empathy. "I am going to really watch how much food I take at the cafeteria back home and try not to have to throw stuff away."

A few of the students were already thinking differently, due to our interaction with the people of Chimbote. I appreciated that.

Charles, the volunteer coordinator, arranged for our weekend activities. I had asked about booking a boat to take us to an island off the coast for swimming and relaxing. I'd seen a brochure in the Gringo room, and Charles said he would set it up. We arrived at the dock after a crazy ride in our rented "chicken bus," as the students called it. The bus looked like it was about to fall apart; all that held it together was chicken wire wrapped around parts of the undercarriage. The seats wobbled and a door often flew open.

Charles walked the students down the pier while I paid at the entrance, although there was not really a gate or tickets. I just handed a man the amount of *Soles*—Peruvian dollars, that Charles dictated. When I got to the end of the pier, students were already loaded into a fleet of tiny fishing boats. "Hey, what about the boat I showed you in the brochure?" I asked.

"That boat leaves from Nuevo Chimbote and is a business owned by a guy with lots of money. These fishermen can use the cash."

I looked at the small boats. Each seemed overloaded with a bunch of my students. The boats rode low in the water, and I did not see any life vests.

"Where are the life jackets?" I asked.

Charles replied, "Oh, they are probably under the seats."

As the students excitedly headed out to sea, Charles and I jumped into the last boat. I could just hear the college administrators chanting "liability, liability, liability." I had no idea whether all of the students could swim. "Hey, keep your arms in the boat and stay seated," I hollered at them. Their laughter assured me that no one was listening.

The boats pulled up onto the island's beach. Feeling very much like castaways, we explored, stretched out in the sun, and devoured snacks. The island was covered with a white chalky substance. Charles told us that it was bird guano. We collectively said, "Eew."

When it was time to go, our boat captains realized the tide had gone out. The boats were stuck in the sand, and we had to push hard to launch the boats back into the ocean. As the waves washed over the students pushing the boats off the shore, I again hoped everyone knew how to swim. Trying to help, I fell, face first, fully dressed, into the ocean when the boat I was pushing lurched into the water. My soggy ride back to the mission did not dampen my spirits, especially listening to the students chatter about the fun they'd had.

The next day, we took the chicken bus up the mountain to climb to the statue of Jesus. I stayed below, watching the students scramble over the rocks and hearing their cheers when they reached the top. Just as Laura had predicted during our site visit, the students loved the excitement of our outings, the thrill of the boat ride and the adrenaline rush of the switchback path up the rugged hillside to the statue. At the side of the mountain, near an open-air chapel, we ate sandwiches, took more pictures and enjoyed the warm sun. Much to my surprise and relief, no one got hurt.

"Hey guys," I said Sunday night at supper, "Let's not mention back home that we didn't have life jackets on our boat trip, or that you climbed up that mountain un-chaperoned. Ok?"

The students laughed and nodded in agreement, then headed off to plan for the next week of classes.

4. Education, Healthcare, and Poverty in Peru: Week Two

A lthough I tried to hold firm on adding more students to our classes, I knew we needed to do something to prepare for additional children who were sure to show up the second week. I collected names on a waiting list, hired local college-age church members who spoke English to help and organized a second course. I also cut the number of teachers in a couple of classrooms by one and moved them into the new classes. Although this re-shuffling of teachers proved a bit chaotic, it gave more children access to our program. Local students streamed into the mission on Monday. Many called out, "Good morning, teacher," in accented but clear English. That alone made all the extra work worthwhile.

The Gustavus students, eager to get back to working with the students, came up with more creative games and activities to expand the use of English. It was clear that both the students and the teachers were having a good time and enjoying the classes.

To meet the demands of adding so many new students, I taught a class of teenagers in the afternoon. Mary taught an additional adult class. When the mission classrooms were full, I led a parade of students to a nearby community center each morning and back to the mission at noon. Mothers picked up their little ones and older siblings at the gate. We quickly became familiar in the community, which meant we could head off to the community center without an escort. Local residents called out, "*¡Hola!*" and waved as we walked by.

Counting students who participated for two weeks as well as those from the one-week classes and the smaller afternoon teen and adult classes, more than three hundred students attended English classes during the two weeks we were there.

Father Jack told us about a local woodworking shop he had established to provide jobs. Workers made simple twin bed frames, among other items. Volunteers who came to work at the mission often purchased the beds, as well as mattresses and sheets, to donate to families in the community.

"The beds meet a real need," said Father Jack. "Unfortunately, due to the fact that family members often sleep together in one bed, incest occasionally occurs."

I had factored in a donation to the mission from Gustavus students as a part of the course fee. I personally felt this might help them to not feel guilty when they had to refuse an occasional panhandler, or someone who made a personal request for money. We purchased bedding and students borrowed tools to build two simple beds. With no box springs available, the bed consisted of a mattress on wooden slats.

The parade wheeling twin beds down the dusty dirt streets of Chimbote on bicycle carts was somber. The college students were silent. A local volunteer intro-duced us to recipient families. We went into their homes and set up the beds, then made them up with colorful sheets and blankets. The students couldn't help but note the dirt floors, woven mat walls and lack of running water and bath-rooms. The grateful words of *gracias* from the families and the smiles from the young children as we tossed them the pillows overwhelmed us.

10. Child from one of the homes where we donated a bed.

When we got back to the mission, we discussed the outing. The conversation revolved around the students' reaction to their brief but firsthand experience with poverty.

"I can't believe that people live in those homes."

"That's where our students live?"

"I was able to give a girl a hug after we set up the bed, but that seemed like so little."

"I feel awful, because we have so much in America."

"What do we do in the face of such poverty?"

"It was uncomfortable, going into their homes and seeing how they live with practically nothing."

"I felt like a voyeur."

Mary and I tried to reassure the Gustavus students that their time in the mission and donating beds made a difference. Supporting the kids in our classes was a positive experience for the local community. Before leaving for Peru, I had assigned the book *Three Cups of Tea* [i] for everyone to read. It's the story about Greg Mortenson's effort to raise money to build schools for girls in Taliban controlled regions of Afghanistan and Pakistan. I believed that college students from Minnesota each had the potential to make a difference in the world. "What you choose to do doesn't have to be as big as building schools," I said, "but it can be something."

The students talked about how their future careers could support others through nursing, teaching, working at a non-profit or volunteering. Once again, one of the students said they were going to make sure they did not throw away so much food in the cafeteria. They would only take what they knew they could eat.

"I feel like such a jerk because I often just toss out half a burger if I had too many fries," someone said. "How selfish is that?"

Not wanting the students to leave their Peru experience with such negative feelings about the problems in the world, I reiterated my earlier comments. "You should feel good about deciding to come here and working so hard to create a positive experience by teaching English to the local children," I said.

The students talked about how they realized they were not producing expert English speakers, but that the children were interested and eager, and how most were learning basic conversational English.

"At least they are off the streets for a couple of weeks," one student said.

"Yeah," another replied, "Walking to the *tienda,* it's hard to watch the kids playing soccer by kicking around an old milk bottle, or just tossing rocks in the dirt. At least when they are with us, they are getting to do some more positive stuff."

Britta, a cheerful nursing student who had assisted during home visits to the sick, added a thoughtful comment about *Three Cups of*

Tea. "There is a quote at the beginning of the book that rings true for our time here," she said. "It is a Persian proverb that says, 'When it is dark enough you can see the stars.' Here in Chimbote, people lead very difficult lives. They struggle to find work. Single mothers raise children on their own with little or no help from out-of-work husbands. Children are forced to grow up and try to succeed in a city where there's very little to hope for. But yet, in the darkness that we are surrounded by here in Chimbote, we are able to see the loving, caring and selfless people that live here much more clearly. None of us will forget the people we've met. We have all learned different, but equally important things from the relationships we have formed."

Following our reflection session, the students came to the conclusion that they would push the idea of working hard in school along with continuing to practice English to their classes. They didn't want the young people to backslide. They wanted to encourage their students to continue with their learning. They wanted their students to practice or at least, remain interested in and be ready to speak a little more English when the next group of teachers arrived.

We decided that on the last day, we would give each student a book in English to keep and read from those we had brought. We planned to send more Spanish-English dictionaries in the next container. We wanted the children to come to the mission library and read, using the dictionaries to look up the words they did not know.

Sister Peggy said that most of the children did not have any books in their homes, so this idea felt good. She said, "School is not a priority for most families. If the kids are interested, they go to school. We try to provide the materials they need, but your ability to motivate these children to focus on learning, English as well as other subjects, will have a huge impact."

We had our stronger Spanish speakers prepare a short speech that the rest of the teachers could read in class. Their words would articulate this idea of ongoing learning and encouragement to our students. With this positive plan of action in place, the Gustavus students said they felt more confident.

As we prepared for the rest of our second week, I suggested that we might use one of our final days of class to take the kids to the beach. I wanted to provide the local children, who didn't have many fun outings, a day at the ocean.

The city beach was badly polluted, and no one could swim in it. So, even though they lived by the sea, most of our students had never been to the beach. I felt they really deserved a trip. Thanks again to Brian and his foundation, we had funds to do something special with the local children. With his support, we had money for busses to take the children to a clean beach.

My college students were not as enthusiastic as I was. I tried to promote the idea. "It'll be a lot of fun. You will all get to spend a day at the beach."

11. Headed to the *estero* houses.

Brandon replied sarcastically, "Sure, let's load one hundred or more kids onto busses, get them to the beach, keep track of them, feed them, keep them from drowning and get them all home safely. Yeah, sure, that sounds like fun."

"I think it would be crazy to take that many kids swimming," another commented.

I reminded them that we had come to Chimbote to take on challenges and try to make a difference. "While it's easy for us to go swimming or have a holiday at the beach, we'll be providing a new experience for many of these kids. It will be challenging, but it's doable."

After a little coaxing, the idea caught on. We decided to make the beach trip a Thursday event for all the morning students. Not all students attended every day, which was somewhat of a problem in providing continuity to the lessons.

We planned to teach beach words in English the next two days, so that we could try to have an English only day. Our Spanish majors wrote out a permission slip that parents needed to sign and return. We planned for Friday, the final day, to follow up on our beach vocabulary and to celebrate our time together. Elise, our art teacher, created certificates that we would give out on Friday, certifying completion of the two-week English language program.

Father Jack had a little farm where he raised chickens and turkeys to feed mission volunteers. He said we could pick out a couple of turkeys, and Mujura would roast them for us so we could make sandwiches for the children. Mary and I perused pens at the poultry farm and picked out two fat birds and carried the turkeys back to the mission by their feet, alive, flapping and squirming. I told Mary there was no way I could wring the bird's neck. She asked the mission guards to kill the birds for us, and they agreed after laughing at our squeamishness.

With the birds plucked and roasted, Brandon, who worked at a restaurant, sliced up the birds. We created a sandwich assembly line, putting together the turkey and bread. Students cut open the buns, stuffed the meat in the bread then stored sandwiches in plastic bags. Voila! Turkey sandwiches to go. We also bought watermelon and Inca Cola for lunch at the beach. The Gustavus health care students would supervise at the beach, manage lunch, keep kids hydrated and put on sunscreen. The rest of us would take turns keeping the kids safe in the water.

I borrowed a large coil of rope from Father Jack to make a perimeter for the students to stay in while they swam. I figured that we could have four students act as posts, holding the rope and creating a swimming area. It seemed like a good idea. As a former lifeguard, I was a bit concerned about being able to check on who was in the water. After thinking about this for a while, I got out permanent markers and gave them to the teachers. I told them to mark one hand of each of their students with a big X as they got on the bus. We would ask them to raise their hands to check on them. We'd know they were our students by the X.

A few of the students thought this day at the beach was going to be relaxing. However, the Peruvian children were so excited, I knew it would be difficult to keep track of them. Every teacher had a list of students and parental permission slips in hand as they ushered their students on the buses. We crammed the buses full, with two or three children on each seat chattering excitedly. Everyone screamed when we went through a tunnel in the rocks as we approached the ocean. They all cheered again when we reached the beach. We knew it was going to be a good day, if not a relaxing one.

We kept track of any student who got out of the water or walked away by asking, "*Levantan las manos*—Raise your hands," so we could see if they were ours by the X on their hand. The health care students chaperoned those who needed to use the bathroom and herded back anyone who tried to wander off. I chuckled to discover that the children would not urinate in the ocean. There were more trips back and forth to the pit toilet than I had expected.

Four Gustavus students stood in the water at the corners of an imaginary square, holding the perimeter rope. I told them, "Make sure no one goes past the rope." I thought we could manage the group by containing them, but the kids kept ducking under the rope or running in and out of the water. We were constantly checking hands.

In some ways, it seemed like a regular day at the beach with a group of kids. However, as we looked around, you could see the differences. Many of the children did not have swimsuits. They paddled around in shorts and tank tops. Very few actually knew how to swim, so we kept them playing in the shallow water. A group of kids gathered small shellfish from the rocks and piled them into their towels. When asked why they were doing this, they explained they were taking the shellfish home for dinner. Not like a typical day at the beach in Minnesota.

Keeping the rope perimeter in place was a challenging job because of the waves buffeting everyone. We rotated students in and out of those positions. The water was chilly, and the waves lapped up into the student' faces. There was also a potential threat of jellyfish washing onto shore, or into a student.

Some of the teachers and health care students made sandcastles, tossed a Frisbee with the children, or sat and chatted with the teenagers. Luckily, we had enough food. It was almost like the miracle of the loaves and fishes, as we passed around sandwiches, wedges of watermelon and small glasses of cola. After we fed them and let them play in the water some more, we checked our lists to start herding the children back on the buses.

Watching the children reluctantly climb onto the bus, Julio ran up to me. "Hey," he said, "I have one kid missing."

A stab of fear ran through me. This is what I had been afraid of.

A catastrophe. A missing child. I panicked. How did someone get past our barrier and our check system? I had some of the teachers put the students on the buses and took another group to walk the beach next to the water. I was afraid of what I might find. Luckily, Julio, with his proficient Spanish, talked to a few of the adults on the beach. He found our student with her parents. They had come to the beach to share the rest of the day with her. They seemed to have missed the part in the permission slip about traveling to the beach and returning home with the group.

After my heart stopped pounding from the thought of telling some distraught parent that I had lost her child, or let them drown, I relaxed into the motion of the bus. The sounds of laughter and English phrases floated around as we headed back. All of us were exhausted, and many dozed on the way home. Parents eagerly greeted their children when we got back to the mission. We all felt good about surviving the trip. During dinner, we reviewed the day. Several of the students commented, "That was really a crazy idea, taking that many kids to the beach."

"Yeah, but they sure had fun," someone responded.

The students agreed that despite the anxiety of watching all those kids on the beach, they felt a sense of accomplishment for providing them with such a fun day. As dinner wound down, the students quieted, thinking about tomorrow, the last day of teaching. They headed off to plan games and a bit of a celebration to close out their time at the mission.

The teachers were concerned because when they told their classes earlier that week that Friday would be our last day, some of the Peruvians were upset. The little ones asked when the next class would start, not understanding that the last day meant an end to their relationship. The teens demanded to know when the group was coming back. "I need to be able to speak English," they said.

The younger children grew very connected to their teachers, so when we got up on Friday morning there was a heavy feeling among the college students. I had planned for Hector to send a bus the next day to take us back to Lima, then on to Cusco and a visit to Machu Picchu. The visit to Machu Picchu would be a reward for the students' hard work. The tour would also help us learn more about the history and culture of Peru. Somehow in my communication with Hector, things got messed up. His bus appeared at eight o'clock Friday morning instead of on Saturday. I tried to negotiate with the driver, but the bus was paid for and ready to go. We would have to leave a day early.

This change was really upsetting to my students. "We can't go without having our final class and saying goodbye!" they pleaded.

I called Hector, and he said we needed to get back to Lima that day because our flight to Cusco was scheduled for early the next morning. If we wanted to go to Machu Picchu, we needed to be back that night. I begged to delay the departure and asked that the bus wait until after the morning classes with the younger children. If we waited until after lunch, the afternoon class teachers might have time for a quick goodbye. We'd be sure to give everyone who showed up an English book from our resources to take home and practice.

At the end of the morning classes, we couldn't get the students to leave. There were tears from both groups as the college students said goodbye. The children hugged their teachers and begged them to stay, saying that they needed more English classes. "We will miss you," they cried.

We finally shooed the young people out of the mission and ate a quick lunch. Afterwards, Father Jack gave us an overwhelming goodbye speech. Some of the afternoon students, having heard through the grapevine we were leaving, showed up for more hugs and goodbyes. We handed out books to the afternoon students and gave the rest of them to Sister Peggy to distribute. Then we climbed into the bus and headed to Lima.

The bus trip was unusually quiet. I suggested that students put their thoughts into their journals while the experience in Chimbote was still fresh in their minds. Looking around at the somber faces, I wondered if the emotional impact of their work at the mission was too much. The connection between the Gusties and the people they'd worked with was strong, considering how short our time here had been. These powerful emotions were hard to manage. I noticed the sad faces and looks of irritation focused on me as we rolled along. I had messed up, and we had to leave before they were ready. As the college students quietly wrote down their thoughts, I hoped for a more upbeat experience in our final days.

5. Heading to Machu Picchu

Traffic was heavy on the long bus ride back up the coast to Lima, and not as exciting as the trip to Chimbote. Hector sent a hired bus, which was cheaper but did not serve food or have a bathroom. The students were starving by the time we had inched through traffic, unloaded our bags and got situated back at the Hostal Gémina, where we had stayed when we arrived. Knowing the area, I went across the street to a pizza restaurant to get dinner while everyone else headed for the restrooms. After two weeks of predominantly Peruvian food, the students inhaled the pizza. We had an early departure in the morning, and after the emotional toll of our quick exit from Chimbote, we were exhausted and crashed shortly after dinner.

Saturday morning, we got up early and loaded into a bus heading to the airport. Hector joined us along with his fiancée Julie and Julie's niece Olga, age fourteen, and Julie's nephew Daniel, aged seventeen. They had never been to Machu Picchu, even though Hector often made arrangements for tourists to travel there. The Gustie students were pumped up after coffee and rolls, excited to explore the land of the Incas.

We would travel by plane to Cusco, the starting point for anyone wanting to see Machu Picchu. Cusco sits 11,150 feet above sea level, an elevation that caused altitude sickness for many visitors. After my experience during the site visit, I checked with my doctor who prescribed Acetazolamide to enable me to avoid the painful symptoms of altitude sickness. I urged the students to get this medication as well, but most of them did not. Many of their doctors told them to wait and see if they experienced altitude sickness before taking the medication. I knew I needed it and prayed that the pills would help me avoid the painful migraine headaches and nausea that had plagued me on my earlier visit. I was supposed to start the medicine two days before we reached the higher altitude. With our unexpectedly early departure, I started a day late. "This drug better work," I thought to myself. "I don't think I can manage things if I have to deal with altitude sickness."

We arrived at the Lima airport only to find that it was raining in Cusco, which meant that small tourist planes could not fly because of low visibility in the steep mountains surrounding the village. After rushing to get everyone up and on the bus early, we sat and waited for several hours before finally taking off. A few of us dozed a little in the hard airport chairs. It was frustrating, but the students played cards and retold stories from our weeks in Chimbote.

Chatter and excitement grew as we started the boarding process. We had to go outside and up a set of stairs to the plane. The students laughed and waved. Accustomed to jet bridges, not an outdoor set of boarding stairs, they students took a ton of selfies. They were definitely more cheerful than the previous day. I was looking forward to seeing Machu Picchu again too, and hopefully I would be able to enjoy it more than I did the first time I visited.

We landed in Cusco after a short flight, walked into the airport and saw attendants offering oxygen to tourists. We wove through the crowds and gathered our suitcases. Hector guided us to our bus, which took us to Hotel Ruinas.

The architecture of the older, local hotel impressed the students. Some giggled at the fact that they were given coca tea made from the same plant that cocaine is made from. Coca tea helps to settle nerves and avoid altitude sickness, though the students were confident they wouldn't get sick. Just to be sure, Hector insisted that we all take a rest and lie down for a couple of hours to allow our systems to adjust. So, after a light lunch, which was another precaution against altitude sickness, we climbed into our beds and tried to rest.

I checked with the students two hours later when we gathered to tour the archeological sites in the city. Most were doing ok. Jenna said she was feeling a bit woozy, but still wanted to come along. Even though it was raining, no one wanted to miss the opportunity to explore Incan ruins. I carried my umbrella. The students clomped along in ponchos. A few students were beginning to feel the effects of the high altitude and sat down to rest whenever they could.

We started at the Basilica Cathedral of Cusco, a beautiful structure that amazed everyone. Students smiled when they saw a painting of the Last Supper depicting Jesus' disciples as native

Peruvians. We were all familiar with the meal shown in the painting, *cuy*—guinea pig.

We walked through drizzle to Qorikancha, the former Inca temple dedicated to the sun god, and learned about the Inca structures built out of huge, interlocking blocks of stone. Guides explained that the original gold panels decorating the stones were taken by the Spanish conquistadors. However, the walls remained thanks to the stonecutting skill of Incan masons. We all struggled to comprehend the Spanish conquest that destroyed the Incan civilization.

A bus took us next to Sacsayhuamán, a fortress of massive stones and expansive terraces. Construction at the site of pre-Incan ruins began under an Incan emperor in the thirteenth century. After Sacsayhuamán, we stopped at Tambomachy, a system of aqueducts where water seemed to flow out of the rocks. Our last two visits were to Puka Pukara, a military guard post used by Incans, and to Qenqo, an Incan temple. The students rolled their eyes and some shivered as they listened to the stories of ritual deaths and blood sacrifices that were carried out in the Qenqo cave.

The Gustavus students were duly impressed by the ancient structures. "These sites are so amazing, with all those huge rocks placed together in such tight formations," one student commented; "how did they do that?"

"Yeah, these buildings are so cool, I can't wait to see Machu Picchu," said another.

While we enjoyed the tour, the long day was taking a toll on some of us. We decided to head back to the hotel to rest before dinner. Hector had more in store for us—an evening at a restaurant known for its amazing Peruvian buffet. We enjoyed all the dishes we'd first eaten in Chimbote, and more. Students seemed to enjoy the *Ceviche* and blue corn pudding, but the rich, sweet desserts had everyone going back for seconds. It was fun listening to local music and watching the dancing. Some students even jumped up to try a few moves.

Although not everyone was at one hundred per cent, the students all wanted to try the Peruvian alcoholic drink that came with our meal. I suggested that alcohol was not the best choice at this altitude, but they ignored me and downed Pisco Sours, toasting each other as they did. Many had at least one bottle of Coke, something they had missed for two weeks. Not everyone was feeling great, so we left a little early to get a good night's sleep before our morning train ride.

Jenna was still not feeling very well on Sunday, so I asked hotel staff for an oxygen tank. Jenna breathed through the mask for about fifteen minutes until her oxygen levels adjusted. I was relieved that the treatment helped her. We ate breakfast and packed overnight bags. The hotel would store our suitcases until we returned. Traveling lighter, we headed off on the next leg of our trip, Machu Picchu, elevation 13,000 feet.

The town of Aguas Calientes, often called Machu Picchu City, sits in a valley at the base of the mountain below the site of the most famous Incan ruins. Two rivers wind through the little town, Río Alcamayo and Río Aguas Calientes, for which the village is named. The popular hot springs provide a place for tourists to relax, sore and tired after climbing to visit ruins. Small houses and shops cling to the mountainside and the riverbanks. The larger Urabamba River skirts the town, with only a small road and levee wall between it and riverside buildings.

The only way to get to Aguas Calientes is by train from Cusco or hiking twenty-six miles up the Inca Trail. Some of the students said they would like to hike, which takes four days, and we didn't have the time. Our plane home was scheduled to leave on Tuesday, so we would have return to Cusco, fly to Lima, and then get our flight home at midnight.

We arrived at the Cusco train station and discovered chaos; crowds of people were everywhere. We had tickets for the train, but when we arrived to board at eight Sunday morning, the lines were already long. After the first train left, we moved up in the queue. Hector asked around and learned that the trains were behind schedule due to the rain. A small mudslide had fallen on the tracks. Porters reassured him, "Don't worry, we are taking care of the problem and clearing the tracks."

I found out later that there had been more than a little mudslide on the tracks. A fairly large slide had occurred overnight because of heavy rains in recent days. The hillsides and mountains were saturated. Workers cleared the track before trains were allowed to leave. We crowded onto the small platform and waited, in the rain, for the next train to depart.

Eventually, the porters began filling the trains a little more quickly. Even though everyone had a ticket number for a particular time, they were putting people on just to get them seated regardless of the time stamped on their ticket. Watching the attendants ask for travelers to hurry up and get on the train, I began to have my first feelings of unease. All the chaos, waiting then rushing around, shoving people onto trains, was not the way things had happened on my site visit. This was not going the way I wanted, but Hector reassured me and urged patience from all of us.

Finally, our group shuffled forward next to the door where people were boarding. We were joined by the guides Hector had hired for the Machu Picchu portion of our trip, Javier Vera and his brother Cris. These men were Peruvians from Cusco who led hikes on the Inca trail for backpackers and gave tours of the site. They were good looking young men, dressed in jeans and t-shirts, jackets tied around their waists. Their dark hair was slick from the rain, but they didn't seem to mind the weather.

"We're glad we got through the crowd in time to join you on the train," Javier said, his dark brown eyes serious behind his glasses. They both smiled and introduced themselves to the students, shaking hands and making sure they met everyone. Javier asked if the students were ready to go, promising an exciting tour. Cris added that he was happy to answer any questions the students had along the way. Their earnest welcome put us all at ease.

Hector, Mary and I stepped back, allowing the students to board led by Javier and Cris. When I finally climbed the steps onto the train, an attendant put up her hand and said, "No." I made a circling, inclusive motion, pointing to the students, myself and Mary, indicating that we were together.

I held up the group tickets and said in my broken Spanglish, "*Todo personas tengo boletas por la similar tiempo.*" I wanted the attendants to know that we had tickets for the same departure time in the same coach. After a confused look from the attendant, Hector followed up my attempt with rapid fire Spanish. The official held her ground in front of the door and would not let us board. With the delayed trains, we could see they had filled the car with other people who were waiting from earlier departures. There wasn't room for all of us.

Hector, Mary, Kyle J., Brandon and I moved down the line, trying unsuccessfully to board another car on the train. The same thing happened at every car we tried to board. The train was full. We couldn't get on. We ran back to the car where the students had boarded. Hector argued some more with the ticket taker, but they closed the door in our faces and the train started up.

The students stared out the window at us wide-eyed. The five of us were ushered back onto the platform and quickly absorbed by the crowd. I elbowed my way forward, jumped down and ran next to the track, shouting at the students through the window. "Stay with Javier. We will meet you at the hotel."

I waved and smiled reassuringly as the train sped up, hoping I looked more confident than I felt. I took a deep breath to calm myself and thought, "Nineteen of my students are heading off to Machu Picchu, and I'm not with them. I'm supposed to be managing things, but I'm just standing here watching the train move down the tracks without me. Oh, man. What do I do now?"

Hector argued our case and we got on the next train headed for Aguas Caliente. I stared out the window watching water crash against the riverbanks with a thunderous roar.

When Laura and I took the train on our site visit, I noticed that the riverbank was very close to the railway. There wasn't much space between the river, the tracks and the side of the mountain. The stream was quiet and calm on my first visit, so the ferocity of the water this trip surprised me.

I felt a few twinges of anxiety. The deep river moved frighteningly fast. Still, I didn't think there would be any risk to the tracks or to our journey, even with the ongoing rain. Hector seemed unfazed. He read his newspaper as we rolled along, so I felt reassured.

The railway to Machu Picchu traverses a narrow track that cuts through the Andes, providing access to the ruins. The first section of the ride would take us along the Urubamba River and through the small village of Ollantaytambo. As I had already traveled this route, I knew that from Cusco, the train would continue through a narrow valley situated between two mountains. One of the mountains was the site for the famous Incan ruins of Machu Picchu. The tracks sliced through the narrow ravine, just barely clinging to the side of the mountain.

Even with several unexpected stops, which we suspected were to clear mud from the tracks, we arrived only forty-five minutes after the students. A few met us at the train station. They were concerned because I carried all the money, the college credit card, and our tickets, which were under my name. The students had been settled into their rooms in Hotel Santuario, a nice place on the river front. Some had napped, but Javier kept them close, anticipating our arrival. The students seemed glad to see us. We heard the relief in their voices.

"That was crazy. The train took off without you!"

"We weren't sure when you'd get here."

"Javier and Cris took care of things for us."

"Are we going to eat soon, I'm starved!"

I smiled. Hunger trumped fear any day.

12. Gustavus Adolphus students at Machu Piccu, January 2010.

With the delays, two trains and the rain, we arrived mid-afternoon in Aguas Calientes and decided to grab a late lunch at a place Javier recommended. The restaurant was a bit touristy, meaning, more expensive. It offered non-native food like burgers and fries, the

Gusties' go-to comfort food. Lunch helped calm their nerves after a hectic morning. The sun finally came out and the warmth cheered us all.

The students were excited to be able to explore and wanted to buy souvenirs, so I suggested they head to the local market after lunch and check things out, keeping in mind two rules: Number 1. No one went anywhere alone; and Number 2. Everyone had to rendezvous with Mary and me at a set time. Students were responsible for getting dinner on their own. I cautioned them to stay on the main road, as the restaurants there catered to tourists and would have food that was well prepared and safe.

That afternoon, they spent their time and money purchasing Peruvian knit hats, Alpaca sweaters and other local items to take home. When we met for a check-in that evening, it was raining again. I worried about our trip up the mountain in the morning. Hector and Javier had decided to get us tickets for the first bus to Machu Picchu to be sure we got ahead of the crowds. The guides reassured us that we would go up even if it was raining. We told the students to be sure to bring their ponchos and reminded them about the early wake up call.

Mary and I sat in the hotel lobby, which had a wall of windows that looked out over the street and the river beyond. The roar of the river was amazingly loud, and as I watched, I noticed massive amounts of water slam against the rocks and the stonewall levies on both sides of the river. I thought, "That doesn't look good." I looked up at the sky. The dark, angry clouds produced a heavy torrent of rain. My stomach tightened, though at that point I had no idea what impact the heavy rainfall would have.

The hotel had one internet connection that took about ten minutes to load. I logged on to the college server and sent a message to Carolyn, the Director of International Education. Carolyn was new to her position and I wanted to let her know that we had arrived safely in Aguas Calientes. The students had been sharing their experiences on the internet, so I wanted to assure Carolyn that everything was ok, despite train departure issues and rain.

I concluded my email message, saying, "The river here is a little high, it's close to the train tracks, and I am a bit concerned. If anything happens, I will let you know. Everything will probably be fine, but I'll let you know if anything changes."

As I was typing, I noticed out the hotel lobby window something on the road that ran between our hotel and the river. There was a little strip of grass on the far side of the gravel road, then a wall, then the roiling river spewing water up over the banks. I saw a manhole cover popping up and down, and water shooting up from underneath. The metal cover tipped up on one side and rolled around. Water spurted out and it plopped back down into place. This happened over and over. I sat there thinking, "There must be a lot of pressure coming through that water system to make a manhole cover bounce like that."

I pointed it out to Mary and said, "That does not look good."

We sat there quietly for a few more minutes watching the manhole cover do its dance. It felt ominous, looking through the dark window at the manhole cover popping up and rolling around. The rain continued to pour down. I thought about what our guides had said about needing to go up the mountain early to get the best views and avoid the crowds. Javier and Cris probably knew that with all the rain, the road could be bad, and they wanted to be sure we got to see Machu Picchu.

The tourist trade was the livelihood for Hector and our guides. The economy of the town depended on tourism, the marketplace, the many restaurants and the hotels. Everyone was invested in getting us up to Machu Picchu safely, so I stopped worrying.

Later, when the river flooded, people said that they knew the situation would be bad, and that we would probably have difficulties. Somebody asked me whether or not I would have gone to Aguas Calientes if I'd known what was about to happen, that I would end up stranded with twenty-one college students in a small Peruvian village. I replied that I'm not sure what I would have done had I seen the future.

Sitting there watching the river, I figured that Hector and Javier and Cris would not put us in danger. I pushed away my qualms. The irony was that if we hadn't left Chimbote because of the bus mix up a day earlier than we had planned, we wouldn't have even made it to Machu Picchu.

6. Stranded: Sunday Morning

We got everyone up at six a.m. Despite another early morning, the students were excited about seeing Machu Picchu. Jenna was still a little sick from the altitude, so Hector and I took her to the hotel next door because they had an air tank. I sat with her while she inhaled oxygen in deep breaths. I looked around. This was a more upscale hotel. The lobby was full of mostly older adults speaking what sounded like German. Tension was in the air, a feeling of anxiety among the tourists milling about, carrying on low, intense conversations. I wondered if they were getting ready for the trip up to Machu Picchu as well.

It was raining when we left the hotel, and it appeared that it had been raining all night. We pulled on our ponchos and walked down the muddy street to the vans. The switchback road up the mountain was almost as bad as the one in Chimbote, with the added fun of having the van's tires spin in the mud when the driver shifted gears on the turns.

"At least this van isn't held together with chicken wire," someone said.

It was still raining when we arrived at the drop off site. Hector, Javier and Cris oriented us and cautioned us to walk carefully on the rock paths because of the constant, misty drizzle. As we rounded the corner that opened up onto the site of Machu Picchu, the students suddenly stopped and stared. The view was simply beautiful. Green terraces stepped down to the valley. Llamas and alpacas grazed in the misty morning. A mountain loomed behind, providing the iconic view of Machu Picchu. Structures that made up the ruins were formed with stones tightly fitted together without any mortar. Hundreds of rock steps led up and down the terraces. Even though I had seen it before—granted, through the fog of altitude sickness—Machu Picchu seemed entirely new and breathtaking.

Javier gave us a wonderful tour. He showed photos and told stories about the discovery of the site and speculation as to why Machu Picchu was built.

"No one really knows the exact purpose, or exactly how the Incas moved the huge rocks and fitted them into place so tightly," he explained. "Archeologists think Machu Picchu was built as an estate for the Inca emperor Pachacuti in the fifteenth century."

"An American historian and explorer, Hiram Bingham, 'discovered' the Machu Picchu ruins in 1911. Bingham believed Machu Picchu to be the birthplace of the Incan society, the legendary lost city of the Incas."

Javier continued, "Bingham thought it was a place for holy women, the Virgins of the Sun, because most of the Incan remains found first were women. Plenty of male skeletons were found later, so we know that Machu Picchu wasn't just for women."

There weren't many people around on the drizzly morning we visited. I was glad we got up the mountain early so we could enter the various areas without being crowded by other groups. We trekked around the site and checked out the ruins constructed of stones that abutted each other so perfectly you couldn't fit a pin between them. I know; I tried.

We all agreed that the buildings were fit for a king. Many believed that Machu Picchu had been constructed as a royal retreat. "Other scholars believe that because it sits in the Andes where the sun could be observed and worshiped, it was a spiritual retreat, a holy place," Javier said.

Our guides provided a lot of information and answered all questions. When someone asked about the theory that aliens had helped to build the site, Javier replied, "That is something we cannot speculate on. But who knows? We really do not know much about this site other than what I have told you, because the Incas left no written records."

Our exploration followed narrow footpaths along the side of the buildings. For those of us who didn't like heights, this part of the walk was scary. There were no handrails for support, no ropes cording off dangerous drops. I found myself pressing up against the wall as we made our way around the side of one of the buildings and encouraged those who were struggling to take it slow and steady. I wondered how I had done this same walk while battling altitude sickness the year before.

The tour was interesting, but long. Mary had been struggling with a bum knee. The steps were especially painful for her. I suggested that she stop and rest. I would sit with her and we would catch up in a bit. But she insisted on seeing it all. Cris walked with her the entire way, offering his arm to support her up the steep parts.

We did not hike the entire five miles of the site or climb all 3,000 steps that link the areas of Machu Picchu, but by the time we were through, it felt like we did. I finally had to ask Javier to take a break, as I could see that the students were getting tired and their attention was waning.

"The students would like to take pictures," I said.

Javier knew the good places to snap photos, and soon everyone started taking pictures and selfies. Because Machu Picchu is 1,600 feet above the river valley below, the views were stunning.

Halfway through the tour, the rain stopped, but it was still misty. The sun came out and the temperature quickly rose. This was good, because I had worried about the rock steps and the slippery paths we had yet to take. I considered not doing the final hike up numerous steps to the Caretaker's Hut, a site that gave a wonderful view of Machu Picchu and the surrounding mountains. The students definitely wanted to climb to the top, and Javier promised we would. He also suggested they come back after lunch and hike to the Sun Gate, the entrance into Machu Picchu from the Inca Trail.

When we reached the Caretaker's Hut, there was stunned silence as we surveyed the view.

"Wow." "Amazing." "Cool."

I heard sighs of amazement as we looked around and saw how high up we really were.

Mary sat down, looked at me and said, "This was worth it. I have always wanted to see Machu Picchu." She smiled but winced in pain and rubbed her knee.

I was thankful for the guides that Hector had hired for us. It was clear that Javier and Cris went above and beyond what was normal guide duty.

Around ten thirty, the students began to ask, "Is it lunch time yet?"

"No," I replied, laughing. Many of the students always seemed to be hungry. It was a constant the entire trip, and that same question had been repeated often over our two-week stay in Peru. "A little longer, just enjoy the view!" I replied.

We had tickets for the eleven thirty slot at the Peruvian buffet. Around eleven fifteen, I asked the students if they were ready to leave the scenic Caretaker's Hut. They hustled down the rock stairs, talking about how famished they were, because, after all, they had been up since six in the morning.

I went into the restaurant and looked around, remembering when Laura and I had been there the year before. It had been packed at the time, but we were just about the only ones there this time. I thought, "This is great. No food lines."

Hector and his family sat down with us, but the two young guides disappeared. I had wanted to pay for their lunch, but they left as soon as we filed in to eat. I didn't know at the time that they went down to check the bridge across the river because they were concerned that it might not still be there. We stuffed ourselves with the various Peruvian dishes and I went back for seconds.

About an hour later, Javier and Cris hiked back up to the restaurant. I invited them to sit down and eat. "I'll pay for your lunch, it's the least I can do. You two have done such a great job," I said. I noticed that Javier looked nervous and Cris was wringing his hat in his hands. I wondered what that was about, but looked away to take another bite from my still-full plate.

Javier tapped me on the shoulder and said, "Deb we need to go."

"Why?" I asked, although I could see the worry on Javier's face. I pointed out that we weren't finished eating. I wanted to be sure they ate their fill. "You said the students would have another hour after lunch to explore. We still have time." I turned away and looked around the restaurant. I noticed that while we were eating, the place had cleared out. That seemed odd. I felt a twinge of concern.

That concern only increased when Javier took my arm and said, "Deb, we need to go now." I looked at my watch and hesitated. Javier insisted, "Really. Right now!"

I glanced over at Hector. The look on his face scared me. I surveyed the place again and saw that we were almost the only people there besides the servers. I recalled thinking how lucky we were that we didn't run into big crowds of tourists.

Our tour had been very open, with lots of room to walk around and examine the various aspects of Machu Picchu that Javier pointed out. When Laura and I first visited, the crowds made the tour feel claustrophobic. We often had to wait for one group to exit a space before our guide could take us in and explain the area. "Why is it so empty today?" I wondered.

I looked at Hector again, who nodded in response to my questioning look. "Okay," I said. "Let's get going folks." I motioned for the students to finish up, realiz-

13. Crossing the bridge over the raging Urubamba River.

ing that something was going on. From the way Javier and Cris urgently ushered the students outside to the vans, and their whispered conversation with Hector, I knew something was up. The students wanted to know why we had to leave. Many protested that they wanted to explore on their own.

"What's going on?" Julio asked. "I thought we could go back and climb around some more."

Hector explained, "We need to head down right away because the river is rising. Javier and Cris went down and checked the crossing." I thought about the way the river had looked when we were on the train and felt sweat break out on the back of my neck.

Javier added, "We need to get going before the bridge is washed away or we won't be able to cross back to the hotel and the train station."

That got everyone moving. We clamored into the bus and the driver started off slowly. Hector and Javier kept talking to him all the way down. When we got to the bridge, we could see the river pounding the piers holding the bridge in place. The water was so high it almost reached the road. The driver stopped and shook his head. He refused to drive the van across the bridge. I was not surprised because the bridge looked pretty unstable with water smashing against the abutments and deck.

The power of the water was frightening. Trees clogged the river. Debris piled up against the bridge structure. Local police were there. They had already blocked off the bridge so no vehicles could cross, even if the driver had wanted to try. There was a suspension footbridge next to the vehicle bridge. Javier shouted over the roar of the river. "We need to walk the rest of the way." He pointed to the footbridge, which was also getting battered by the water, causing it to sway as the river roiled underneath just inches from the deck boards.

I looked at the students' frightened faces and back at the river. It was a scary sight—branches and debris swirling around and banging into the bridge supports. The thought of walking across the swaying planks suspended over the powerfully rushing water was not something I wanted to do.

Trying to sound confident, I said, "Maybe we should all hold hands and cross together. That might be safer."

Josh replied, "No way, the weight of all of us crossing together could cause the bridge to fall."

"Ok, then let's go one at a time," I said, stepping slowly out onto the bridge and feeling tremors from the rampaging river shake the deck boards. Trying to stay calm, I took a hesitant step, then another, hoping to demonstrate that it was safe. I gulped a deep breath to relax my nerves, stopped and waved for the students to follow. Josh walked tentatively onto the bridge, moving slowly down the center, staying away from the rails. The rest of the students followed. Some crossed the bridge with quick steps in a rush of excitement. Others shuffled cautiously across. The occasional sound of the wild water and things smashing into the bridge was scary. A few students crossed with a partner, holding hands. When everyone, including Mary, had made it across the bridge, I brought up the rear.

On the other side, I turned to Javier and asked, "What now?"

"The road on the other side of the bridge, the one that leads back into town, is pretty much underwater. It's been blocked off by the police," Javier explained. "We need to follow the train tracks on this side of the river to get back to Aguas Calientes. The rails run closer to the mountain, higher up and away from the water."

"All right," I said. "Let's go."

We climbed up a low hill and onto the tracks. I hollered to the students, "Watch out for trains," unsure whether or not trains were still running.

The tracks, carved into the rock, wound along the side of the mountain, snaking through several tunnels. The lush foliage and

14. Walking the tracks back from Machu Picchu.

cool rock softened the roar of the river. After a while, the sun reappeared and created a beautifully warm day that made for a nice hike through the Andes. Singing and chatting and laughter from the students told me that they were enjoying the walk.

Mary's leg ached. She struggled and moved slowly. I told the students to walk at their own pace, that we would catch up to them at the hotel. Julie and Hector stayed with Mary and me as we plodded across the railroad ties. The sun grew hotter. We followed the curve of the tracks into Aguas Calientes and wound up close to our hotel where the students who'd arrived ahead of us waited.

I looked around, wondering what was going on. I could see people scurrying in and out of buildings carrying furniture and bags. When we got closer, it was evident that the river had eroded the riverbank and the levee wall had crumbled. The little strip of grass next the road was almost gone. The river inched closer to the steps of our hotel.

We walked close to the buildings to keep as far from the river as possible, stopping when we saw a huge tree begin to wobble. The torrent stripped away the last bits of earth from the roots before it suddenly crashed into the water, sending a powerful spume high into the air. The uprooted tree smashed into boulders and tumbled down the gorge, pushed by the powerful river. I had never seen such fury in a body of water. It was frightening.

When we reached the hotel, some of the students ran up to us and said that the workers at the Santuario were emptying the building to protect things from the flood. All of our bags, packed and ready for our departure, had been taken to the main plaza. We made our way to the central square. I was not happy to see all of our backpacks just sitting out in the open with no one watching them. A few of the students had already picked up their bags, others were sitting around talking.

"Is everything here?" I asked, searching for my stuff. I'd left the airplane voucher and the train tickets in my backpack and was relieved to find that nothing was missing. I shouted for the students to gather their backpacks and check in with me to make sure we were all together.

"Ok" I said, "We are on the two o'clock train, so we need to get going. Grab your stuff and let's head out."

7. Stranded: Sunday Afternoon and Evening

I started walking toward the train station around 1:45 p.m., hollering over my shoulder at the students to hurry. Javier and Cris, who had been standing off on one side of the plaza, ran over to me.

"Thanks for helping us, you guys," I said to express my appreciation for what great guides they had been. I put out my hand to shake with Javier. He stepped back and shook his head, a worried look in his eyes.

"I'm sorry," he said, "but there is no train."

"No train?" I didn't understand what he was saying at first.

He repeated, "There is no train."

"What do you mean there's no train?" I dropped my backpack. "What happened?"

"First the rain created mud slides. Then, as the river got higher and more powerful, it tore out the tracks," explained Javier. "The intensity of the water twisted the rails. There are gaps where tracks should be. You will not be able to leave on the train."

I glanced at my watch then stared at Javier. "So how long will it take to fix the tracks? We checked out of the hotel. We have to get back to Cusco tonight."

"I am sorry," Javier said, shaking his head. "It is not possible."

I looked at my watch again trying to estimate how long we could delay and still get back to Cusco in time to catch the plane for Lima. "When will they have the tracks fixed?" I looked at Javier, incredulous. "What are they doing to fix this? We need to get back."

Hector interrupted. "Deb, it could take months to fix the tracks." Reading the shocked look on my face, Hector continued, "This is Peru, not the U.S. Things like this take time."

"You will stay here tonight, and we will figure things out," Javier added.

"We only have our backpacks and overnight stuff," I exclaimed. None of this was making any sense. I looked at Mary who just shook her head. "We need to leave," I said. "There has to be something we can do."

I had no game plan, no idea what to do. I began to panic. My stomach lurched and I sucked in a big breath. The reality of our situation suddenly hit me. I could feel my heart racing.

This disaster had just been waiting to happen, what with the rain and the geography of the area. We were in a precarious situation from the start. Hector and Javier surely knew that the river might flood. Still, they did everything they could get us to Machu Picchu. Maybe if we had left for Cusco earlier in the day, we wouldn't have gotten trapped. But then, Hector, Javier and Cris wouldn't have been paid for our tour. I wondered, "Did they let us stay when they knew we could be trapped here? Would they do that?" I shook my head, disgusted at my negative feelings. I was overwhelmed, frightened and angry that I had allowed myself to get into this situation.

The students crowded around, listening to what Hector and Javier had to say. They looked at me and Mary for answers. I just stood there, my thoughts churning. Then questions began flying.

"How are we going to get home?"

"How long will we be here?"

"What about our flight?"

"What should we do now?"

"I think I should call my parents."

"Oh my god, we're trapped here!"

I could see fear and apprehension in the students' eyes. I frantically searched my mind, trying to think of what to say, but nothing came to me.

Javier jumped in, "First, we are going to get you a hotel for the night."

He was the only one thinking straight. Javier sent Cris up the hill into the village to find us a place to stay. "We will need to wait and see what happens," he continued. "It is not just the train tracks. Many buildings and homes may be washed away. There are also lots of tourists in town who are in the same situation as you."

"What are you going to do, Javier?" I asked. "Can you get home to Cusco?" I realized with a guilty pang, that I had only been thinking of myself and my responsibility for the students. Of course, there were others with even more to lose than us. Local Peruvians would suffer most because of the flood.

While we were all standing there, a helicopter swooped low over the village. Julio looked at me with a grin and said, "Wow, a helicopter ride out. This is the greatest course, ever!" He started to head toward the village where the helicopter had landed. "I think they're coming down in the soccer field," he said, "Let's go!"

Javier grabbed Julio's arm. "Wait," he said, "We don't know what's happening. There could be a lot of people and confusion when the helicopter lands. Let me go check it out first."

The students shrugged. Some sat down on the edge of the fountain in the plaza where our bags had been dropped off. Some sipped water.

Javier took off at a trot. No one really had much to say, but everyone looked nervous. I took a deep breath and smiled shakily at the young college students around me and considered ways to get back to Cusco. There weren't many options, so I made a mental list of all the things we would need if we were going to stay in Aguas Calientes another day.

Bottled water was a big deal. We couldn't drink the local water. Toilet paper was also in short supply in most bathrooms, much to the student's dismay. We would need to buy water and toilet paper. I pulled out my money holder and counted my Soles only to realize that I didn't have much cash left.

We were all happy that Javier wasn't gone long at the soccer field. He said that a group of older people hired a private helicopter to get out. "Authorities are bringing down lots of backpackers from the Inca Trail," he said. "All of the hikers are looking for a way out as well. The soccer field is surrounded by people who wanted to get on the rented helicopter," he continued. "There's a fence around the field with only one entrance, and the police are keeping crowds out. There's a lot of pushing and shouting. When the helicopter landed, the people who hired it, twenty older men and women, all white, hurried over from the sidelines, got on quickly, and took off." Javier looked at me seriously. "There was some shouting about Americans getting to leave first. Some said that if you have

15. The main square in Aguas Calientes.

American money, you can buy your way out." He added, "I don't think the group was American, but it is not good over there now, not so safe. We need to stay away from the soccer field for a while."

Crowds in the plaza grew larger. A lot of people arrived on the last train, and hikers came down off the mountains. No one was going to Machu Picchu.

"Vans are not crossing the bridge to the site," said Hector. "We were one of the last groups allowed to visit Machu Picchu, and among the last ones out." Hector continued, "You were really lucky to go to the site because not many vans left this morning. People came thinking they were on an overnight, in and out after one night. Now all of them are looking for hotels."

Fortunately for us, Cris arrived back with news that he'd found a small, local hotel, the Royal Inte, that still had rooms. It would hold all of us. "The hotel is located in the upper part of the village, across the high bridge in the center of town and up a steep street. Others haven't found it yet," he said.

Hector took my elbow. "Come on, Deb," he said, "let's get everybody settled into their rooms."

We walked up behind the main road onto a back street that wound past small *mercados* offering local snacks and beverages and up through the village at a steep angle. Huffing and puffing in the low oxygen, we stopped out front of a small hotel. I checked everyone in. The desk clerk handed out keys and the students—two to a room as usual—went to settle in. Mary and I also shared a room to ensure there was room for Hector, Julie, and her niece and nephew.

The Royal Inte Inn was a backpacker hotel, unlike the hotel we stayed in the night before. Things were smaller, the construction was simpler. I noticed a sign announcing that the Royal Inte only took U.S. dollars, and only cash, which caught me by surprise. The room rate was a bit high as well.

The clerk looked at me, expectantly waiting for payment. I didn't have the cash so I asked Mary to tell him that I would get the money and be right back. "While I'm gone, Mary, find out what we can do for dinner."

"Don't worry, Deb," Mary replied. Then she chatted with the owner in Spanish.

Hector and I went to a nearby ATM. When I put in my card, a notice in Spanish said the machine was out of money. We trekked across town to another ATM, but it was also out of cash. When we saw the line at the final ATM, we were hopeful. But by the time we got to the front, people shook their heads. "*No dinero.*"

I needed $990 to stay the night, and I didn't have nearly enough. When we got back to the hotel, the Gusties were sitting at tables in the dining area. Mary asked the kitchen to make pizza to provide comfort food. It was clear that we had taken most of the rooms. The desk clerk again looked at me expectantly. I explained that I wasn't able to get cash. "*No dinero a las ATM.*"

I did have my college credit card, and I waved it at him. He shook his head to indicate the hotel didn't take credit cards. He pointed to the sign and said, "*Sólo dólares americanos o Soles.*"

I didn't have the cash, and the students were already checked into their rooms. I had no intention of bolting in the morning without paying." I told the manager, "I'll be right back with the cash." Then I gathered the students and said that we were going to need to open "The Bank of Deb." We had to pool money to pay for the hotel.

Sarah H., an accounting major, was nominated to be our bookkeeper. Everyone pulled out their cash. We collected Soles and dollars the students had stashed away for the trip home. Sarah H. created a ledger with everyone's name and their contributions, as well as a repayment column. I assured the students that as soon as I got money from the ATM, I would pay them back.

We had planned to pay for meals from our class account. Because of this, most students didn't have much cash. I took what money I had and deposited it in the Bank of Deb. I was greatly relieved that we pulled together enough cash to pay the desk clerk for our rooms that night, plus a little extra.

Holding back the price of pizza and beverages, I passed out funds to students to go scout markets. I suggested they buy bottled water and toilet paper. Groups of students left to hunt for what we needed, while the restaurant prepared dinner.

I sat for a moment to consider our predicament. How long might we be trapped in Aguas Calientes? I dug through my backpack for the cell phone the International Director had given to me for just this type of situation, a flip phone with a cumbersome battery charger. I hadn't had time to call the college, what with the crazy pace of returning from the mountain and finding out we were stranded. My call would have to go through the college operator to connect, but the phone didn't hold a charge for very long, which made it troublesome. I searched for a place to plug in the charger. The only outlet was behind the front desk, so Mary explained what we needed to do. I held up the phone cord for emphasis.

The space behind the front desk was narrow and required me to contort and wriggle to plug in the phone and make the call. When I reached Carolyn at the college, I explained what was going on.

"We're out of money and none of the ATMs are working. If you could bump up my credit limit, that would be good. Then we'll have enough for whatever it takes to get out of here. I'm hoping I'll be able to get cash from the ATMs tomorrow."

Carolyn said, "We heard about the flooding and have been waiting to hear from you. Don't worry, the college will extend unlimited credit. Just keep the students safe and fed and make sure they have a place to sleep." The show of support surprised and pleased me. "When do you think you'll get out?" Carolyn asked.

"Not sure," I replied. "Hopefully, tomorrow."

"I'll need to re-book your tickets for your flights home," said Carolyn. "As soon as you have specific information, let me know. If there is anything you need us to do, just call."

"Ok." I hung up thinking, "I'm not sure that the college can help us. Besides making sure the credit card doesn't max out, there's really not much they can do. We're on our own."

The students came back with their treasures and we divided up the loot so every room had water and a roll of toilet paper. We devoured the pizza. I suggested that the students work on their final course reflection, which was due at the end of the trip. They responded with a lot of grumbling. "Hey," I said, "the course requirements are still the same, and you all have a final paper to write."

16. The flooded Urubamba River from the hillside north of town.

Alison, ever the perfectionist, was adamant that her brain could not provide a deep, reflective assessment of her experience in Chimbote under the current circumstances. After a moment to considered Alison's remarks, I told them to write what they could; I would accept their reflections with no judgment, no failing grades.

"But you have to turn in something. That's your task for the evening." I shooed the students off to their writing with one more task. "You'll need to stay in in your rooms or the lobby. No leaving the hotel."

Hector pulled me aside and said, "Deb, I haven't been able to find out anything. We need a plan. I think it's time for you to call the embassy."

I stood there stunned for a second. "The U.S. Embassy?" I asked dumbly.

"Yes," said Hector.

My notebook with all the emergency contact numbers and student health cards were in my luggage at the hotel in Cusco. I swore silently to myself. The notebook was heavy. I didn't want to carry it on such a short trip. "I don't have the Embassy number," I said.

"I do," Hector replied.

Of course, he would have the number! Hector had managed many tours. He knew what to do when something went wrong. I was glad he'd come with us. I sighed with relief knowing I would have laid awake all that night worrying about what to do. Calling the Embassy was a great idea. I was sure they would have a plan to get us out.

Instead of using my cell phone, I followed Hector to a telephone center where local residents paid to make calls. My thinking was off. I felt sluggish and slow. The stress made it difficult to comprehend the magnitude of our situation.

It was pouring rain again when we tramped out into the night. I only had my umbrella. We slogged down several streets in the dark. I got progressively wetter and colder. The hard downpour splashing on my ineffective umbrella left me feeling miserable. I needed to find myself a poncho.

When we arrived at the phone center, Hector explained what I needed to the operator. The cost per minute was kind of pricey. In order to save our cash. I first tried to use my credit card. No deal. The operator wanted dollars up front. I had to pre-pay for whatever amount of time I thought the call would take. I guessed it might take ten minutes and passed the operator a handful of Soles. Hector gave me the number, which I repeated to the operator who connected me to the American Embassy in Lima.

After listening for a minute, I rolled my eyes at Hector. "Crap! It's a recording."

The message provided me with options. One of them was a

number to press if I was experiencing a life or death situation. I didn't think we qualified for that level of response at this point.

I whispered to Hector, "I asked to be connected with an Embassy operator."

"Get someone high up to talk with," he replied.

I took a deep breath, wanting to be professional and calm. I explained to the person who answered that I was in Aguas Calientes with twenty-one college students. "We have a flight to catch tomorrow," I said. "We need help because we can't take the train back due to the flooding."

The person on the phone replied, "I need to get the duty officer," and put me on hold. I made a face at Hector. While I waited, the Embassy phone system played old 70s music. Minutes ticked by. I had to pay for more time, peeling bills out of the stash in my pocket and handing them to the operator.

When the duty officer answered, I explained everything again, and she told me that the State Department official in charge was not available. "We'll get back to you tomorrow," she said.

I tried to stay calm. "I have twenty-one college students here and no access to money. We need help getting home."

"You'll need to wait until tomorrow."

"How will you get ahold of me?" I asked.

Hector, sensing the call was about to end, whispered loudly. "Deb, you need to be more excited."

"What?" I asked.

"You need to be more excited. Let them know this is a big problem."

I thought for a second. Then I dropped any sense of calm, raised my voice to a hysterical pitch and shouted into the phone. "I don't know what to do! We don't have any money! We don't have any way to get out! I have twenty-one American college students to take care of and I'm afraid someone might get hurt. What am I supposed to do?"

Hector encouraged me, "Keep it up."

I reined in my voice a bit and took another deep breath then repeated, "I am here with twenty-one students. Can you tell me how I should handle this?"

Hector interrupted again, "More excitement, talk with more excitement."

"You have to help us!" I cried, sniffing and trying to force some tears, hoping my performance would get us some quick action.

Hector gave me a thumbs-up.

The duty officer reassured me that she would take my message to the consulate officer. "We can call you in the morning or you could call us back," she said.

I shouted in earnest. "How am I supposed to call you? I don't have a phone." With all the stress, I completely forgot about my cell phone.

Hector passed me a slip of paper with a number on it. "Give her my number," he said.

I rattled off Hector's cell number. "I need to know that you can help us. I don't know what else to do. How am I supposed to keep these college students safe?" I ended in a panicky voice.

When Hector typed the Embassy number into his cell phone, he looked at it closely then put the phone into his pocket. "I don't have much battery power left, and no charger. I need to call my travel company office tomorrow and see if there's anything they can do. We need to get more cash and call the Embassy from this phone center in the morning."

"Right. Get more cash. That will be easy," I answered.

It was about nine-thirty in the evening, and I was completely exhausted. Thinking about what to do next overwhelmed me. On the walk back I noticed a sign across the street from the hotel that said "Massages—50 Soles." I was feeling pretty stressed and told Hector I was going to get a massage to get the kinks out. He said he'd let Mary and the students know. I thought a massage would be a great way to relax. Luckily, they took credit cards.

My massage started with a woman rubbing my back in circular motions. It was not unpleasant, but not really helping my tense muscles. Then she judo-chopped me all over my back like an old-time cartoon character performing a massage. Evidently the training for masseuses in Peru is different from in the U.S.

"Ouch!" I said, hoping to get a more comfortable treatment. The chopping went on for what seemed like forever. The women were very friendly, but I spent thirty minutes there and it was not very relaxing. The massage actually hurt more than it helped. Still, it was nice to get away from everyone for a bit and think about out predicament.

I wandered back to the hotel in the dark and the ever-present rain. "How much more water could this village and the rivers take?" I wondered. "How are the people of Aguas Calientes going to handle all this rain?"

Some of the students were playing cards in the lobby. Others were talking and sharing stories. Julio and Brandon, both considering political science for their majors, ran up to me seemingly unconcerned about our situation. Their boyish faces were damp, and they grinned excitedly. Brandon's glasses were steamed up from the rain and heat.

"Hey," said Julio, "we overheard people talking out in the streets when we went to search for water."

Brandon cut in excitedly, "The Argentinians are having a rally in the plaza. It's supposed to start about now. Let's go!"

"Political history in the making," Julio added.

They were almost out the door when I grabbed Julio's arm. "Oh no," I said, "We're all staying right here in the hotel for the rest of the night. We can play Celebrity.

"But the rally could be really interesting," said Julio. "I can translate for you."

"It could also be dangerous." I replied. "A lot of folks are upset about the helicopter taking out a few white adults, saving themselves and ignoring the needs of everyone left behind. Attending the rally might just stir up bad feelings. We need to be more careful and gracious while we are here. We don't want to be seen as ugly Americans." I continued, "The people who were camping in the mountains have no place to stay and no money. We have both. What might we look like to people who have to sleep on the streets?" I looked around at my students and raised my voice, "No one goes out after dark unless I say so," I said. "Stay away from the main plaza and the river, both could be dangerous. And the number one rule is no one goes anywhere alone at any time. Ok?" I stared at them knowing my voice had been stern. There was uncertainty on some of faces. "Look, I don't want to scare you, but it's just better to be cautious. Why don't you all get to bed. We need to be ready to roll tomorrow morning after I get in touch with the Embassy." Heads slowly nodded in agreement and students wandered off to their rooms. I was pretty confident we'd manage to get out the following day. Surely the American Embassy would have a plan.

Exhausted, I headed up to the room Mary and I shared and fell into bed. Mary was reading. She had brought a small C-PAP machine to Peru to provide her with oxygen while she slept, but she'd not packed it for our overnight trip to Machu Picchu. "I'll be fine," she assured me, and soon fell asleep.

I tried to drift off, but Mary's breathing often seemed to stop. She would gasp. Then she would continue inhaling. I listened for a while. At one point, I almost shook her to be sure she was breathing. I tossed and turned, worrying about Mary, wondering what I would do if she stopped breathing during the night. I listened a while longer to make sure there wasn't a problem. Mary's loud exhales let me know she was indeed breathing.

Ideas rolled through my head. The students were pretty stunned by our plight. What could I do to help them cope? I felt unsettled myself, and my stomach did its usual nervous tightening. What if we couldn't find a way to get back to Lima? How would village residents manage to survive? The stranded tourists? Were there sufficient resources for everyone? Food? Water? Thoughts rattled around, keeping me awake. I could usually figure out what to do in challenging situations. That night I was clueless. My shoulders ached from my massage. My feet hurt from our long walk back to town. My stomach continued to roil. Mary's breathing echoed in the little room.

I lay there awake, resolved to remain calm and maintain a positive outlook, vowing to be as upbeat as possible. I didn't want the students to see my fear and uncertainty. I needed to set an example for them. Despite all that had happened that day, my concern about Mary, and my worry about what the morning would bring, exhaustion finally took over and I fell asleep.

8. Stranded: Monday Morning

I slept soundly the rest of the night but woke early the next morning. Of course, college students being college students, they were all still sleeping. Mary and I dug into the hard rolls and coffee provided by the hotel. The round bread we typically ate for breakfast in Peru, called *roseta*, was crispy on the outside with a soft, airy interior. We had eaten this bread every morning in Chimbote, along with the other delicious breakfast foods that Maruja made for us. Now there was only the bread, with a little butter, and coffee. Hector joined us. Julie and her niece and nephew were also still asleep. The three of us drank our coffee in silence, thinking about what we might face that day.

Javier and Cris wandered into the hotel lobby. I never knew exactly where they were staying, or when they would appear. They had told us they were originally from the area and knew lots of people, so I figured they were well taken care of. We had only paid for them to lead our Machu Picchu tour. Seeing them again, I wondered how much of their service extended to our current situation—would they hang around and offer their help or would they take off and leave us to fend for ourselves? More importantly, given our financial uncertainty, would I need to pay them to help?

Javier and Cris knew Aguas Calientes well, which was comforting. They said they had scouted the ATMs and one bank was allowing people to withdraw a limited amount from their machine. The line was long, so when I said I needed to get some cash, Cris ran ahead to hold my place in line. I followed Javier to the bank. Cris was already pretty far up in the queue, so I avoided a long wait. The ATM was dispensing the equivalent of one hundred fifty dollars. I thought that would get us through the day. We turned back to the hotel. Angry voices from people still in line told us the ATM had run out of cash again. Many were turned away.

The Embassy hadn't called by the time I got back to the hotel, so I asked Hector if he thought we should go back to the phone center. He suggested it would be cheaper if we got coins and used a pay phone he'd discovered while exploring the village that morning. I exchanged paper Soles for coins at the front desk and followed Hector through winding streets. We arrived at the only public pay phone in the village to discover a long line of people waiting to make calls. When my turn came, I called the Embassy. A consulate officer named Sara answered immediately. I gave her my name, explained our situation and Sara replied, "You're the one who called last night. They said you sounded pretty upset."

Good, I thought to myself. I got them to pay attention. "Yes, well, I am concerned about what we should do," I said, doing my best not to come across as hysterical on this call. "Last night was upsetting. I didn't get much of an answer." I started to restate the problems we faced.

Sara interrupted, "I need a list of all the students and their passport numbers." Assuming the Embassy might want passport numbers, I had the students list their name and number the night before. I didn't want to hang up, afraid I wouldn't be able to reconnect with her if I did. I was also worried I wouldn't have enough change for the call. I began to rattle off the information. Hector fed coins into the phone whenever I ran short of time.

Sara interrupted and asked, "Where the heck are you guys from?"

"Minnesota," I said.

"Hmm," she responded. "You'll need to spell those names."

I went through my list again, spelling all the names, repeating passport numbers. I was about to finish when Hector tapped me on the shoulder.

"Am I on your list?" he asked. I looked up and could see the concern on his face.

"Sure," I replied, "Give me your ID."

I told Sara that I also had four people from Peru who were traveling with us. "They need to get out with us as well."

She said, "I can't guarantee that".

I replied with urgency, "They have to come with us. I can't leave them here. They're our support system."

She said again, "I can't guarantee it."

Hector looked at me, his dark eyes full of worry. Feeling protective of him and a bit agitated, I replied belligerently, "Well, I'm not going without them."

Sara paused. Hearing no response, I changed direction. "What's going to happen next?"

Sara ignored my statement about Hector. "I have your names, passports, that's all I need," she replied. "We'll coordinate this with our people. We have access to a couple of small helicopters used for drug patrol. They each hold six passengers. We're going to start taking out Americans. After that, we'll stay and work with everybody else. As soon as we can, we send in the choppers. Put your students in groups of six and have them ready to go. We may need to move fast."

"Where are we supposed go?" I asked.

"Just listen for the helicopters," she said. "We probably can't use the soccer field. We heard it wasn't really adequate for the helicopter that landed there yesterday. We'll land somewhere behind the resort on the far side of the river. Go through the train station. Follow the path behind the last resort. You can't miss it. That's probably where we'll be. Just listen and be ready to go as soon as you hear us."

I took a deep breath. The plan seemed vague and a little sketchy, but I didn't have any other options. "Ok," I said, "we'll be ready."

Hector said, "Deb, I don't have a way out. Julie and me and the kids, we need to come with you."

"I know. I'll make sure you leave with us," I said. Truth was, I had no idea what to do if the Embassy refused to evacuate Hector and his family. I wasn't sure I'd follow through on my threat to stay behind. Still, it didn't feel right to abandon Hector. He'd stayed with me, been my support all through the chaos. His calm demeanor helped me stay cool and collected. Hector had suggested I call the Embassy in the first place. I felt unsure, conflicted, and hoped I wouldn't be forced to make such a decision.

We headed back to the hotel and found the students hanging out in the lobby playing cards and chatting.

"Hey, guys," I said. "I got ahold of the Embassy. We need to organize for helicopter pick-up." Just then, Hector's phone rang. It was Father Jack. Hector handed me his phone. The priest told me he'd heard about the flood and tracks washing out. Everybody at the mission was worried about us. He said he called the Embassy to let them know our group was most likely in Aguas Calientes and the Embassy confirmed they'd made contact with us.

Father Jack said, "Folks at the Embassy said you gave them an earful last night. You must have been pretty forceful, Deb," he chuckled. "They told me they have a plan to get you out."

I didn't want him to know I had resorted to hysteria. "I just wanted to be sure they understood our situation, that's all," I said. "Thanks for the call."

"Remember that in Peru, things move slowly," he said. "We'll be praying for you."

"I think we might need those prayers," I replied. I started to ask him if he knew anyone in Aguas Calientes who might be of help, but before I could finish, Hector's phone died.

I looked over at the students and sighed. It was time to get organized. We needed to create groups of six. While the students were coping relatively well, I worried about some. I didn't want anyone to panic. A few had had prior experiences managing tough situations, and I hoped they would be a calming influence on the others. I grouped more experienced students with those who might need support.

I set up three groups of six students, each with a group leader. Another group had three students plus Julie, Olga and Daniel. Hector, Mary and I could follow in a group with other stranded Americans.

"Team leaders," I said, "you need to make sure your group stays together. Be sure you get on the helicopter together. If we stay in our teams, we'll know where everyone is and no one will get left behind." That was the wrong thing to say.

"What?" someone said in a panicky voice, "You think there is a chance somebody might get left here?"

"No," I replied. "But just like field trips, we need to make sure everyone is accounted for. The team system will keep us organized. We need to look out for each other. No one gets left behind. Make that our mantra." I gave everyone a reassuring smile. "We wanted an adventure, didn't we? Well, this is it." I continued, "Here's the deal, we board the helicopters in teams, and we'll rendezvous wherever they take us. Ok? Whoever lands first, wait for the other teams to arrive."

The students nodded in agreement. The teams conferred among themselves to be sure everybody was ready. Hector suggested we head over to the train station to situate ourselves closer to the helicopter landing. We passed through the market. Swarms of people crowded around the train station entrance.

"Wait here while I check things out," said Hector.

People huddled on the stoop in front of shops on a side street and fanned themselves. It was already hot. There wasn't much shade as the sun rose over the mountains. At least it wasn't raining, but we had no idea how intense the sun could be in the mountains. We crowded into a small slice of shade provided by the buildings, dropped our backpacks and leaned against them. I asked a couple of students to buy more water so that everyone had their own bottle. I handed over most of my cash. After I assured them we would not leave before they got back, two groups headed off.

Hector maneuvered through the crowd at the train station to look for our path once we got to the gate. About the time the students returned toting twelve-packs of bottled water, the sound of a helicopter startled us. Everyone jumped up. Hector waved us back. "There are a lot of people down there, all wanting to get out," he said. "It's really crowded. Everyone is packed in tightly. They're all trying to be the first to leave. I'm not sure who's in charge or how we're supposed to move through the gate." Hector continued, "There are many people waiting for a train, or whatever way out they might have. The entire area around the gate is crowed with people. We'll have to go through the congestion when the Embassy helicopters arrive."

The train station was surrounded by a fence topped with razor wire. It also had a double gate, padlocked shut, the same gate that had been wide open when we arrived. A small doorway in the middle of the gate stood open. The narrow entrance created a bottleneck as hundreds of people tried to push through.

"Aren't the helicopters for us?" I asked. "Sara from the Embassy said to be ready when we heard the helicopters." Hector shrugged. "They must have a plan," I said. "Let's give it a try."

"It's very chaotic, Deb," cautioned Hector. "Let's just take one team and see how it works."

We took the first team of six students to the gate. I was shocked by the size of the crowd. Everyone was anxious to get out of town.

Hector said he'd heard there were more than fifteen hundred people staying in the village, all of them there to visit Machu Picchu or hike the Inca trail. Backpackers sat on unrolled sleeping bags and leaned against the train station fence. Many of them had spent the night there in hopes of heading out early. The crowd was young, most in their twenties. A lot of them were South American, visiting Peru on Christmas break from the universities.

We quietly edged into the line, moving as close to the front as we could. It felt uncomfortable. People were giving us the evil eye. I wondered how many had heard about the private helicopter. Hector pointed out a sign written in Spanish. "If you have American money, no worries! You will be rescued!" The sign appeared to be a reaction to the hired helicopter. I started to feel nervous about the Embassy plan.

When we finally heard the helicopter, I assumed it had been sent by the Embassy, just as Sara had promised. The mass of people at the train station also heard the helicopter. Local police appeared and tried to control the situation, urging the crowd to be patient. But as soon as the gate opened, a mob near the front pushed through and rushed toward the sound of rotors.

There was a lot of pushing and shoving and yelling. People tried to wedge their way through the small doorway. After struggling to limit the number of people exiting, the police forced the gate closed. We had maneuvered closer to the gate and were suddenly surrounded by the pulsing crowd. We heard some taunts about Americans. Bodies pressed against us as people continued to surge toward the gate.

I was scared. People sometimes got trampled in similar crowds. When the gate opened again, would we make it through or get shoved aside? People were staring at us. There were many blonds in our group. Most of the Gustavus students were white-skinned, and white skin stood out in the crowd. I could see the fear on our students' sweaty faces. Hector looked around and whispered loudly, "Let's go back and wait until the crowd is calmer."

With so many eyes glaring at us, we carefully inched through the mob and herded our students back to the side wall. Once back around the corner with the rest of the group, we flopped down in the sliver of shade and gulped water. We heard the helicopter whirring overhead, the sound fading away as it left carrying its human cargo.

Hector reminded me that the Embassy owned several helicopters. He was sure another one would arrive. We decided to wait a little longer. After a while, I sent Julio to check things out at the train station gate, violating my rule of no one going anywhere alone.

Julio was perfect for the reconnaissance. A Latino college student with excellent Spanish language skills, Julio fit well into the group of largely South American college-age travelers gathered at the gate. He understood what people were saying. Hector was too old to blend in, and the rest of us were clearly not from South America.

While Hector moved the first team of six closer to the end of the long line, Julio maneuvered through the crowd to see what was going on. The rest of us stayed where we were. When we heard the helicopters again, Julio returned.

"It's crazy down there," Julio said after completing his recon mission. "There's a constant surge of people pushing toward the gate."

Hector looked at me, sighed, and said, "I don't think we are going to get through right now." We watched another helicopter land and listened to the roar when it took off.

Julio said, "After the choppers land, the gates open and people just shove through."

"I thought the helicopters were coming for us," I repeated.

Hector said, "The pilots can't say, 'Oh let's wait for the Americans from Minnesota.' The crowd is too intense. They have to take whoever is next in line."

We continued to watch the choppers drop down, load up, and quickly take off before returning in about thirty minutes from wherever they were ferrying their six passengers. Clearly, it would take a long time for the line to diminish. Getting through the gate and onto a flight was not going to be easy.

We couldn't see the exact landing spot from our location. Julio reported that flight crews weren't just taking people out, they were also bringing food and water for the village and dropping off supplies when each helicopter landed.

I hadn't considered the fact that, with the train out of service, it wasn't just that we couldn't get out, no one could get in. No food supplies could get into the village. And we Minnesotans weren't the only ones trapped unexpectedly. Everyone in the village was experiencing difficulties. I had to acknowledge to myself that we were in much better shape than many of the local residents. Some lost their homes, while others likely had no food or water.

Tourists and hikers from the mountains also needed food, water and shelter. The Embassy told me their goal was to get the Americans out first, then they would continue evacuating people until everyone was rescued. The needs for food and supplies also had to be addressed. I realized that with so many people in the same boat, it was ridiculous for me to think we should be among the first to leave.

The helicopters coming and going, and the people pushing forward into the train station, mesmerized us. I confessed to the students that it was unlikely we would leave that day. They were obviously disappointed. While we were absorbing the situation, Javier and Cris showed up.

Javier announced, "It seems you are not leaving today, so you need another hotel. You also need to find a place to eat."

Once again, our guides appeared with helpful suggestions just when I was unsure of our next steps. Their continued support really impressed me.

Cris lead us down the hill and across the river to a residential area. We passed the infamous soccer field and headed up a narrow street to another hotel.

"Cris, what's happening to your family?" I asked. "And the people of Aguas Calientes, are they getting food and water?"

"Many of us here are from Cusco," replied Cris. "Some may go back there to work. But others own hotels, restaurants and shops. They will want to stay to protect their property."

"Have any homes been destroyed by the flood?" I asked.

"A few hotels and shops by the river may have trouble, but most people live up here, which is where we are going. Most homes away from the river are safe."

Javier added, "The city of Aguas Calientes receives a fee from the purchase of tickets to Machu Picchu. The city government has resources," he said. "I think they will pay for continued helicopter deliveries of food and water. They will want to help residents."

We saw families sitting out on stoops and children playing in the streets, and many eyes followed us as we trudged up the street to Hotel Incanto. This place was small, but Cris assured us it was also cheaper than tourist hotels. Unfortunately, they didn't have the number of available rooms we needed, so we consolidated by putting more than two students in some rooms. The male students volunteered to bunk together in tight quarters.

The custom in Aguas Calientes, it seemed, was to pay before you stayed. I eyed the desk clerk when he asked for payment, knowing I didn't have enough cash. Cris told me that he picked Hotel Incanto because it was one of the only small hotels that took credit cards. The hotel only took MasterCard. The college credit card I carried was Visa. I looked around at the students. "Anybody have a MasterCard?"

Mary Ellen volunteered, "I do."

"What is your limit?" I asked. One night for all of us would cost around three hundred dollars. I had one hundred fifty from the ATM.

"I have a limit of three hundred dollars, and I haven't used it yet on the trip." She replied.

"Ok. Mary Ellen, please go pay our bill." Then I said to Sarah H., "Put in ledger that we owe Mary Ellen three hundred dollars."

I was pleased to see how the students were helping out. Mary Ellen had not complained about having to use her credit card. Sarah H. had willingly taken on the role of our accountant. We got the room assignments and keys sorted out, and everyone settled into their quarters quickly, because, of course, everyone was hungry and ready to head out for lunch.

9. Stranded: Monday afternoon

T he students had identified restaurants that took credit cards when they explored the village the previous day. With that in mind, we went in search of lunch, quickly noticing that some of the smaller places were closed. A few shops also stood empty.

I asked Javier about it. "Local workers are returning to family who live in the mountains," he explained.

"How are they getting out?" I asked.

"They know these mountains," Javier replied. "They are walking out."

We headed back along the train tracks. Near a wall at the edge of the street, a large pot of rice boiled over a big fire. People were lined up waiting for food. Village officials had set up tarp shelters in the main square where people could sleep. I was grateful that the college had provided us unlimited credit, though I worried I might not have enough money for meals. A lot of places just didn't accept credit cards. I was going to need more cash.

My husband, when we were on a camping trip and ran out of cash, had asked a restaurant manager if he could buy money, in addition to purchasing our meal on our credit card. So we got dinner plus cash from the restaurant to tide us over, and charged it all on our credit card.

"Javier," I asked. "Is there a restaurant that might still have cash on hand?"

"Why?" he asked.

"If you can find a restaurant that takes credit cards, preferably, Visa, ask if we could buy cash so we don't have to rely on the ATMs. Do you know anyone who might let me do that?"

Javier thought a minute. "I know the owner of a fancy restaurant that is still open," he replied. "I will go ask if he would be willing to do this. It is a good idea."

"I'll meet you back at the hotel in an hour," I said. "If you connect with a place where we can buy money, we can go get it. And tell the owner that all twenty-nine of us, counting you and Cris, will eat at his restaurant for dinner tonight if I can buy cash." Javier nodded and headed off.

Later, I sent the students out to shop, divvying up the cash from my stash. "We're going to be here for another night," I said. "Spend the money. That way at least we'll help out shop owners who are losing business due to the flood. Avoid the crowds by the train station and down where they're handing out food," I warned. "And be sure no one goes anywhere alone." We agreed they would check in with me or Mary at the hotel at a specific time.

After the students took off, I wandered over to a group of Americans I had spotted earlier, edging into the small crowd to listen to a man, Phil was his name, explaining what the State Department planned to do. Phil worked for the State Department but was in Machu Picchu on vacation. I pushed forward. I wanted to talk to Phil. He said he'd been in contact with the American Embassy in Lima. I piped up and said I'd talked to them as well. Other people said they'd also called. Someone shouted that Phil should be our contact with the Embassy, since he knew people there. That way, we wouldn't all keep trying to connect with State Department officials.

Phil explained, "The Embassy said I should try to gather up stranded Americans to coordinate an exit strategy with the Embassy." Phil added, "Spread the word to other Americans. We're meeting on the bridge, at two o' clock."

I ran back to the hotel and told Mary what I'd learned and asked if she wanted to go or stay and check in with the students. She said she'd stay.

"Tell everybody to stay close to the hotel." I looked up at the sky when I left for the bridge. It was beginning to rain again. I pulled out my trusty umbrella and opened it.

Phil, being a State Department officer, had higher clearance and more connections than us ordinary tourists. He would be the one to get us out. I hustled over to the bridge. About twenty-five to thirty people were gathered for the meeting. I tried my best to appear nonchalant, but I'm sure we all looked suspicious to any local residents passing by. The whole thing felt a bit like a spy movie. I moved in closer.

Phil said he would be our point person, the one the Embassy would communicate with about the situation. He repeated what I'd already heard. The Embassy would fly in more helicopters to take out the Americans. After that, they would continue to help others evacuate. Phil said we needed a organized system to determine who would be leaving when.

Someone suggested we draw names from among those of us at the meeting. When your name was drawn, you would get a number. We would leave in that order. There would be a list of names. The Embassy would have a systematic way to keep track of all evacuees. I explained that I was with a group of twenty-seven, including Hector and his family. I added that we would need to go together. That was met with a negative response from those around me.

"You'll have to split the group up," somebody said. "It wouldn't be fair for all of you to go ahead of everyone else."

"This is different," I said. "I have all the funds and the tickets. This is a college group. I'm expected to keep the group together."

"You'll have to go last," said another person.

"Why is that?" I argued. "It seems to me it might be better to get a large, noticeable group of Americans out of here before there are any problems. The rest of you traveling in pairs and smaller groups aren't as visible as we are."

"No way," came the response.

"You don't get to go first just because you're a larger group," another added.

Two people were tearing paper squares from a notebook and handing them out. Phil said, "Write down your name and the name of your companions, so we can draw your number."

I quickly wrote, "27 college students and faculty—all needing to go at the same time," and put a big "G" on one side so I could see when it was drawn out. We all stuffed our papers into a hat. Someone pulled out the names. Another person, waving a sheet of paper, proceeded to list the names called out alongside their departure number.

When my piece of paper was drawn, the woman who had put herself in charge of the lottery read it and said, "No way." She shoved the paper back inside the hat. I was frustrated that nobody seemed to understand my predicament.

Phil explained, "The Embassy said there are problems getting us out. When it rains, the helicopters can't fly. They have to wait for it to stop. They are also trying to figure out a way to avoid the crowds gathered at the gate."

Phil started talking on his phone, looking around as he spoke. "There's another back gate on hotel property. It leads to the helicopter landing spot. I'm going to check it out. We can meet here again at nine tonight." People nodded in agreement.

Numbers continued to be drawn. My crumpled piece of paper was pulled out again, then put back. It was clear that our group would go last.

I followed Phil when he left, waiting for an opportunity to make my case. He was looking for something, walking around, gazing across the river, talking on his phone. I stayed behind him.

During a pause in his conversation, I announced myself loudly, "Hey, Phil. Hi. Say, I'm a college professor and I'm here with twenty-one college students. We need to leave together." I wanted to make sure that he knew that there weren't just one or two of us. Most of the stranded Americans were in smaller groups. I said more adamantly, "My students and I have to leave together, Phil. That's the issue. I'm not leaving anyone behind. We all have to go together."

He turned around, paused, and looked at me. He nodded and said, "I'll try to work something out," then continued walking.

By this time, we'd stopped in front of a tall, locked gate, the entrance to the area behind the hotel Phil had mentioned. He tried to look over the gate to where the helicopters might be able to land. He started talking again on his phone. I stood up on a nearby rock to try and see. There was someone wearing what looked like a pilot's uniform on the other side of the gate. He also had a phone and appeared to be talking to Phil.

Phil moved forward to enter the gate, but by then we were surrounded by a small crowd who had followed Phil to see where he was going. When he tried to pass through the gate, people began to push and shout, "¡No, no, no, no pasen, no pasen!" They clearly didn't want him to leave. They seemed to think he was trying to sneak out, as if he had some secret connection with the helicopters.

The crowd continued yelling at Phil that he couldn't go through the gate. Some young men blocked the entrance like they were going to push him away. I slid to the side of the group and backed around the corner of a building. Phil edged away from the opening then suddenly turned and quickly strode off through the crowd. I ran around the building in the other direction and came up behind him.

"Hey, Phil," I asked. "What's the deal with the gate? What's happening?"

I startled Phil when I stepped out between the buildings. He jumped, paused to look at me, then answered, "The local people, all the tourists and hikers, they're not happy. They sense we're planning to get Americans out first." He stuffed his phone in his pocket and pushed through the dwindling crowd. We were both still surrounded by a lot of people, but he kept walking. I did too, following right in his footsteps. He looked over his shoulder at me and said, "I'll call the Embassy back and we'll see what else they can do. I'll let everyone know tonight at our nine o'clock meeting."

"Phil," I said, still working to make a connection, "you've been so busy. Have you eaten?"

"No," he said. "I am trying to save my cash."

"I know a place where they take credit cards," I said. "Let me buy you lunch." I figured if I had time to chat with Phil, maybe he would help us to get out as a group. I thought about how my husband often takes clients out to dinner or lunch to try and make a sale. I figured I needed to schmooze with Phil to make my case.

Phil and I had a tasty lunch of spicy chicken and rice, my second lunch that day, as I didn't want him to think I was just trying to butter him up. He told me that his job in the State Department was planning buildings in foreign countries. He wasn't used to emergency situations. He'd come to Machu Picchu between assignments and gotten stuck like the rest of us.

I explained my need to keep everyone together. Phil said it seemed reasonable. "I don't think the rest of the Americans have a problem with that, as long as you are the last group to leave."

I sighed. "Being last to leave means we're stuck here for days. It's one thing for a couple of people to manage for a few extra days, but

I have twenty-one college students. I need to keep them fed and safe. It would really help if we could be the first to leave. Then I wouldn't have to scrounge up money for food and supplies for so many people for however long we're stranded."

Phil said he would talk to the American group about my situation that evening. He cautioned that it might not be possible to change things now that we had drawn numbers for departure. I was disappointed but decided to wait until after our meeting to tell the students about any extended stay. I wasn't finished trying to convince people that our large group really did need to go first.

17. Waiting for news of when we would be evacuated.

When I got back to the hotel, Javier told me he found a restaurant whose owner was willing to let me buy cash. I checked in with Mary and the students, then followed Cris and Javier back up the hill to the restaurant. The place was dark and gloomy inside with no one eating or working. Javier introduced me to the owner and explained what I wanted to do. We went into a back-room office and the owner wrote up a charge slip then rang up a credit card bill for three hundred dollars and handed me the cash. When he imprinted the card number, I felt like I was taking part in some kind of shady deal. The shadowy room and my lack of understanding of what was being said made me nervous.

The passport holder I'd been wearing around my neck contained our money. I stuffed the cash in there. Javier explained to the owner that the group would be coming to dinner later that night. The owner said that I could pay for the meals with another credit card charge. He gave me a nod, confirming our agreement for dinner. I shook his hand and said, "*Gracias.*" The owner seemed very serious and a bit intimidating, especially since he was dressed formally in a suit. He gazed at me with serious eyes as if to tell me not skip out on the meal I'd promised to purchase.

Back at the hotel again, I paid for another night's stay with cash from the restaurant. It took almost all of the money I had. Mary Ellen had maxed out her card, so I was glad I'd gotten cash. I wanted take care of the bill immediately to be sure we wouldn't have to scramble on Tuesday, in the event we needed to leave in a hurry. I felt good about buying cash at the restaurant.

The students checked-in around mid-afternoon. It hadn't rained. The sun was hot and the air sticky. I counted to be sure everyone was there, then asked about their day exploring the village. Some went shopping, but no one had found a place to buy clean underwear, so they'd decided to have a laundry day.

Most of the buildings in Aguas Calientes had an accessible but unfinished top floor studded with rebar and concrete, just like our hotel. Some of the students had washed out their undies in their sink, then carried their laundry to the top floor and hung it on a rope strung between two pipes. Mary and I decided to join in. We soon added to the line of men's and women's briefs, bras and socks flying in the breeze. "There's a lot hanging here," I said. "I didn't know you brought so many clothes with you."

"We didn't," replied Molly, "we're going commando."

"Oh," I stammered, "too much information."

Everybody laughed. It was nice to have something to smile about. We stretched out, the wash flapping in the wind, and enjoyed the warmth of the sun on the rooftop.

I heard more about what the students had done earlier. They'd spent a lot of time watching the river. Someone said, "It's fascinating how the water is carving up the riverbanks. It's powerful and mesmerizing to watch."

"Yeah," said Kevin said. "it's also scary. I heard that people have been swept away. They got too close to the edge and the ground crumbled beneath them."

That horrified me. "You all need to stay away from the river," I admonished. "We don't want anyone falling in."

"We're staying back from the edge," Kevin reassured.

I said, "Don't go down to the river at all." I saw a lot of eye rolling. I felt like a nagging mother but wanted to keep everybody safe, so I made them promise to avoid the river.

Later that evening we gathered to go to dinner. Hector found me before we left. He said he didn't have access to any more money and was worried about his expenses. I put my arm around his shoulder and said that as long as I could cover things with the college credit card, I would provide support. He had been instrumental in helping us get ahold of the embassy, so I felt I owed him. I knew we could sort out all of the costs after we got back home. Hector gave me a hug.

We spilled into the elegant restaurant. The students were impressed. Lovely greenery and sculptures filled the room. There were white cloth tablecloths and napkins and crystal glasses on each table. "Order whatever you want," I said.

They were excited to have a special meal. A couple of students wanted to order alpaca steaks, but the restaurant was out of that native dish. Most ordered the Peruvian favorites: *Lomo Saltado*, a kind of stir-fried beef, or *Ají de Gallina*, a creamed chicken dish. We ordered Ceviche for all of us to share. No one ordered *Cuy*.

The staff brought us complementary pisco sours, a native egg white and pisco beverage. Pisco is grape juice fermented into a high-proof alcohol, a standard drink in Peruvian bars. Not all the students were of legal drinking age, and faculty were instructed to make sure our classes followed the law when traveling, which meant prohibiting alcohol. I had explained all this before we left the States.

The students looked at me over their beverage glasses and I made a decision. "As a part of this course," I announced, "I think we need to have some special coffee. It's a part of the Peruvian culture." Students looked at me questioningly. I lifted my pisco sour, took a drink, and said, "I have a limited understanding of the language. But I think this is a very unique Peruvian coffee." The students laughed and sipped their drinks. The term "special coffee" became our code word to get around the issue when some of the students wanted an adult beverage.

When the food arrived, we were surprised to see our appetizers served with animal carvings creatively designed from vegetables. The students compared their animal totems and took pictures before eating them. There was a lot of conversation and laughter.

Cris and Javier joined us for dinner as well. I asked again what they thought about the effects of the flood on the community.

"It will not be possible to bring tourists to Machu Picchu for a while," said Javier. "Without the train, there is no easy way to get here. Some might still hike the Inca Trail, but most visitors come by train. This is our livelihood. I have been guiding tourists for years, and Cris left his other job recently to join me in the business. I am not sure what we will do now."

Hector added that his tour company set up many tours to the area as well. He wondered how the disaster would affect his business. "There are also all the people who have restaurants here, or who sell in the market. They will be without any income until the tourists return."

I looked around guiltily as the students ate, laughed, and enjoyed themselves. Except for our group, the restaurant was empty. Javier said most of the people stranded could not afford to eat in a place this fancy. "The owner is going to close up tomorrow," he added. "His supplies are low."

I sighed and shook my head. "That's awful."

"Don't feel bad," Javier said. "It's good that you are spending your money here. Waiters and cooks get one more day of pay, and that's important. It may be a difficult time ahead."

While we were eating, we could watch people in the street through a large front window. One of the students suddenly hollered, "Hey, there goes somebody wearing a Gustavus t-shirt."

The main course had not yet arrived, so I said, "Go see why they're wearing a Gustavus shirt in Aguas Calientes. Maybe they know somebody at the college."

Two students took off out the door and ran after the person wearing the shirt. A few minutes later, they walked back in with a young man in tow.

"Oh my gosh!" I exclaimed to Hector, "It's Matt, one of our education graduates." I jumped up and ran over to him. "Matt, what are you doing here?" I gave him a big hug.

"I've been teaching in Chile," he said. "We're on break. So, I came to Aguas Calientes to see Machu Picchu." Matt was a social studies graduate working in South America through a program that placed English speaking teachers in schools.

"Did you get up to the site?" I asked

"I walked up yesterday, so I was able to see everything."

"You walked?" I repeated.

"Yah, cheaper that way," he replied.

"Where are you staying? Are you ok?" I continued.

"Well, I met some people I might be able to stay with," he replied. "I hiked up the mountain with them. I thought I would head back to Chile this afternoon, and of course, I can't do that. Some of the other hikers were going to try and get a room for us to sleep in tonight."

"Have you eaten?" I asked.

Matt hesitated, looking around at our full plates.

"Are you short on money?" I asked. "Are you able to buy meals?"

"I've been getting by," he answered.

"This is the group I brought from Gustavus," I told him, sweeping my arm to indicate the college students. "You're a Gustie graduate, Matt. We'd love for you to stay and tell us about your adventures."

Matt looked at the fancy interior, our plates full of food and animal shaped vegetables. "I really can't afford to eat in a place like this. I'll find something affordable. I was looking for food when your students accosted me."

"No worries," I said. "I'm glad they caught up with you. I have a college credit card, and as an alumnus, I think it is only appropriate that you join us."

Matt looked hungrily at our meals, hesitated, then agreed. The waiter brought him a menu. He looked at it and said, "I haven't had dinner options like this for a long time."

I already was paying for twenty-one students, Mary and me, Hector, Julie, Daniel and Olga, as well as Cris and Javier, so adding Matt didn't seem like a big deal. I knew the college was very loyal to its alumni. I hoped that it wouldn't be a problem when I returned with a large bill for this meal. We'd eaten mainly in modestly priced restaurants, but we'd long since overspent out food budget. We had the ledger for the students' money, and I kept an account of our expenses. But it was hard to track of all the smaller things we bought each day, like water and toilet paper. I hoped to sort it all out when

I got home. Part of my job was to keep track of expenses, and that was becoming difficult.

Matt had developed a high proficiency in Spanish after spending six months in Chile. More Spanish-speakers might be helpful. After dinner, I told him that if he wanted to, he was welcome to bunk with the guys at our hotel. He said he would go check out what his new friends had set up first. I gave him directions to our hotel, and he said he'd come by to let me know if he needed a place to stay.

After stuffing ourselves and enjoying the light-hearted conversation, the students gathered around our table. "What's happening next?" they asked as we prepared to leave.

"Well," I said, "there is another meeting for Americans at the bridge at nine. I am going to go and see what's up. Then we'll meet in the hotel lobby. I'll let you know what I find out."

The students walked back to the hotel with Mary. She'd been limping since we got back from Machu Picchu. Her knee was swollen. I did the running around so that she could rest her leg.

I asked Hector if he wanted to come with me. He said that given the tension in the city, he didn't think he should go to a meeting for stranded Americans. I pulled out the little flashlight from my backpack and headed off.

Americans milled around at the bridge waiting for Phil. As soon as he showed up, we all huddled around him. I think it must have looked pretty obvious to anyone walking by that we were planning something.

"I got word from the Embassy that they definitely want to get Americans out before dealing with all of the people camped out by the train station," Phil said. "We're going leave through the gate behind the Inkaterra Machu Picchu Pueblo Hotel. It's across the river. Just past the side gate is a path to a flat area where helicopters can land. They'll start at first light tomorrow. We're all supposed to be ready to go. We need to do this quickly. There are a lot of people here who don't think we should be getting out ahead of them. But the Embassy has the helicopters to do it, and they want to get us out. We won't have to fight our way through the crowds at the train station. We need to meet in front of the Inketerra gate at four thirty a.m. in the order of the numbers we drew this afternoon. Gather quietly. Try not to create attention."

This meant we were going to sneak over to the landing site under the cover of darkness. The rest of the people trapped here would be unaware of our exit. It seemed like a plot for a movie.

"Don't talk about our plan," cautioned Phil. "Just show up at 4:30 and be quiet about it. We don't want anyone else to find out."

The plan made me nervous, but I figured the State Department must know what it's doing. I walked back to the hotel and found Matt in the lobby, ready to join our group.

"Not staying with your friends?" I asked.

"Too many bodies for one room," he said.

Josh had been sitting nearby. "He'll fit between the beds." Josh said. "We've got blankets he can sleep on."

It made me happy to see the students were being welcoming to our unexpected guest.

"So, what's up?" Hector asked.

"Let's all go to my room," I said, indicating the room Mary and I shared.

Everyone crowded in, students sitting on the bed and the floor. I looked around at the trusting faces eager to find out what was happening. The room was hot. Despite our laundry day, the smell of sweaty bodies and unwashed socks began to waft through the tight space. I thought about opening a window but didn't want our voices to carry. I smiled at the students and plunged ahead with my information.

"Here's the deal," I said. "The Embassy is sending helicopters to pick us up at dawn behind the last hotel on the far side of the river. We need to be there at four-thirty a.m." I looked around and continued, "We need to keep this quiet. Don't let others know what's going on. In the morning we need to get to the gate quietly."

"So, what does that mean?" Alison asked.

"It means we will get up at four a.m., quietly gather our things and head out for the hotel across the river. We'll wait at the gate for Embassy officials to let us through and onto the helicopters when our number is called. With all of the people stranded here, they just don't want us to create a ruckus." I replied.

"I don't know," Alison said, her voice quavering. "It sounds scary. Are you sure we should do this?"

"It'll be ok," I replied. "It's natural to be a little bit scared or nervous. This is a totally new experience. But we'll all be together. I have a flashlight we can use. It won't be so bad."

"But what if people hear us and get mad about us sneaking out," she asked.

"The State Department came up with this plan, so I've got to believe it's going to work. If we move quietly, we can be over there and out to the helicopters before anybody wakes up," I answered. "We can do this."

Hector and Mary nodded in agreement.

I reminded the students about the groups we'd set up. "Stay with your team. I am pretty sure it'll still be six people to a helicopter. We might need to break into smaller groups. There are a lot of other Americans getting on the helicopters. We want to stay together as a group, so we may be at the back of the line, but don't worry, we'll get out. Make sure you stay with at least one other person from our group. No one goes alone, and we don't leave anyone behind. Ok? Everyone gets on a helicopter."

I'd selected the young people for this course after interviewing over forty interested individuals. I'd asked for each of them to describe how they'd managed a difficult event in their past. These students had all given great answers, so I knew they could handle our current situation. Still, I noticed a frightened look on some faces.

I said, "I've been in a scarier situation. I was on a rafting trip. I fell out of the raft and was stuck underneath."

"What?" someone said.

"Really?" asked another.

"Yeah," I said. "Let me tell you about my little rafting adventure. I was really scared, but I knew that if I kept my head together and followed the directions I'd been given by the rafting guide, I'd be fine." I started in with my story. "I accompanied students to Denver on service trip to assist needy residents with house repairs. After a week of service, students got a fun day. We went to the Poudre River for a whitewater rafting trip. As group chaperone, I volunteered to accompany them downriver."

I continued, "We loaded the rafts. The guides numbered students and assigned them to boats. I waited until the end. This is a habit I have for making sure my students are all where they should be. The last few students and I were ready to board when the guide said all the boats were filled. He'd need to use an older raft. Not seeing this as a problem, I climbed in with five students. Our guide gave us directions and we started paddling down the river. There'd been a lot of rain. The river was roiling and boiling over rocks. Kind of like what we have happening here," I chuckled.

"It was challenging to maneuver the raft, and we had fewer people to paddle on our boat. We got high-sided on a rock and tried to push away, but we were stuck. Water began sloshing over the sides and the raft started to fill up. It was an older raft, so there were no ports for self-bailing. Cold water rose around our feet and threatened to sink us. The guide hollered that we needed to get to shore and empty the water from the boat. We finally heaved ourselves off the rock and paddled frantically towards the riverbank."

The guide yelled to me, "Jump out and hold us on shore so the rest can get out."

"Ok," I replied and waited for the moment where we would be close enough for me to jump on shore. The raft spun around and hit the riverbank. I leapt out. The shore was slippery. I slid back into the water. The depth and the force of moving water pulled me under the raft. I got stuck, my face plastered to the underside of the boat, unable to breath."

At this point, I looked around and saw that the students were getting into the story, listening attentively, not looking so scared. "What'd you do?" someone asked.

"For a fraction of a second, I panicked. I felt like I was drowning. Mentally, I took a deep breath to calm myself and tried to recall the instructions the guide had given us when we signed the safety waiver. Ok, don't panic, don't panic, think. Think! Then I recalled we'd been told that the force of the water would keep anyone sucked under a raft stuck there. If this happened, you needed to walk yourself off the underside, hand over hand. I forced one hand past the other, inching forward until I pushed myself off the bottom of the raft and popped out from under the boat like a cork. The current carried me downriver, tossing me around violently. I remembered we'd also been told to keep our feet forward. This way, your shoes would take the brunt if you bashed into the river rocks.

So, I forced myself around facing forward with my toes up. I kept my mouth shut to avoid swallowing the rushing water and careened downstream. Another raft suddenly pulled up beside me, students and one of the other chaperones paddling furiously. Someone reached out and grabbed me by the shoulders of my life jacket. I looked up and was about to shout my thanks when I was shoved down under water. I swallowed a mouthful of river. Just as quickly, I was pulled up again and hauled into the raft. Oh yeah, I thought to myself as I sputtered and choked, remembering the final safety tip. In order to get enough momentum to pull someone back into the raft, rescuers have to dunk you down before they yank you out."

Some of my students laughed.

I finished my story. "I huddled in the bottom of the raft, water rolling underneath me, for the rest of the trip. We finally got to shore in the still water beyond the rapids. I was helped out and wrapped in a blanket. My own two kids saw me sitting there and came over."

"Hey Mom," they said, "wasn't that fun? What an adventure, right?"

"Yeah," I agreed weakly, "Some adventure."

I paused and looked around before wrapping up my story. "Everything worked out. I followed directions. I was rescued. The same thing applies here. Just stay calm. Take deep breaths when you feel nervous or scared. Follow directions, support each other, and we'll all be fine."

There were a few sighs, chuckles and head shakes. Before the students headed back to their rooms, I said, "Make sure you have water for tomorrow." I passed out bottles I'd been hording in our room. "Get some sleep," I said. "It's going to be a short night." When the students shuffled off to their rooms, I motioned for Julio and Matt to follow me.

"I am not one hundred percent sure about the best way to get to that back gate at the Inkaterra," I said. "You two, with your language skills, can pass through the crowds better than the rest of us." I told them I had followed Phil to the gate that afternoon, but I wasn't sure I could find it again in the dark. "I want you to locate the hotel gate and figure out the best way to get there. This way we can move quickly and quietly in the morning. Come back and tell me what you find out." I wanted everybody to have directions to the landing site. I definitely didn't to want wander around the streets at four in the morning with a large group of students.

"Cool," said Julio, "another reconnaissance mission."

"No messing around," I said. "Check it out, come back here and let me know what you find." I knew Matt would follow my instructions. Julio, I wasn't so sure about.

Hector asked, "What about me and Julie and the kids.

"I figure there are going to be so many people, and this is going to happen so fast, that no one will know you are not an American," I told him confidently. "Just make sure you speak English, and tell Julie, Daniel and Olga to stay silent."

Mary had headed to bed. With my best Spanish speakers off looking for our morning route, I grabbed Laura and motioned for her to follow me. Laura was also pretty strong in Spanish. I said I needed her to help me speak to the hotel manager. We went downstairs and I asked her to tell the man at the front desk that I wanted to reserve our rooms for another night. Turned out, he was the owner, so I asked Laura to request that he reserve our rooms. I wanted him to hold our rooms just in case we didn't make it out, but I didn't want to let him know about our four-a.m. departure. I worried that maybe the State Department's plan might not work out. They would be evacuating more than one hundred Americans with only three helicopters capable of carrying six passengers at a time. It would be quite a challenge to get us all out before the other stranded tourists and locals discovered our plans.

Knowing this, I told Laura to tell the owner I would pay for the rooms in the morning. She translated. I gave him three one hundred Sole bills, the equivalent of forty dollars. "Tell him I'll give him the full amount for the rooms tomorrow."

We started to leave, and Laura added a few more words. The owner looked at me with a frown.

"What did you say?" I demanded.

"Just that we were giving him this money because we don't trust that he'll save the rooms," she replied.

"No, no, no," I whispered forcefully. "We want his trust. We don't want to offend him. Tell him that was not what I meant, that you made a mistake. Tell him I said, I want this to be a gift for him because we know he will hold the rooms for us."

"Sorry. I thought I was helping," she said, then spoke again.

This time the man smiled at me, patted my hand and nodded in agreement.

I smiled back, hoping I had made the deal. Back in the lobby, Laura asked, "You gave him a bribe so he would keep rooms for us?"

"I prefer to think of it as a thank you gift for what he is going to do," I said, then shooed Laura up to her room. I went upstairs to a small landing area that had a couch and waited for Julio and Matt.

About twenty minutes later, Matt came back and described the location of the hotel gate. He said he could easily find his way back. I thanked him, and he headed off to bed.

I went to my room, then suddenly thought, "Where's Julio?" I went down to his room to check. I knocked.

"Come in."

I opened the door and immediately felt like I was stepping into a locker room. The stale smell of sweat and unwashed clothes hit me. All these guys were stuffed together in one room with little access to water to keep clean. It wasn't healthy. Still, I was on a mission, and couldn't worry about hygiene at the moment.

I peeked in. They were watching a grainy movie. Julio wasn't there. "Where is Julio?" I asked.

"We don't know," they replied.

Oh boy. Was he hanging around with campers out in the street? I started to panic. Matt came out of the bathroom. He said that Julio was next door talking with some of the girls. I stormed over there and pounded on the door. "Julio," I hissed, "You didn't come back and report about what you learned."

"Oh, well, Matt did that," he replied easily with his ever-present smile.

"I was worried," I said. "I didn't know where you were. I told you to come back and report, and you didn't."

He looked a little sheepish. "Sorry."

"Ok, ok, you're here. No worries," I said, realizing that I must have sounded frantic. I patted him on the back and thanked him for checking things out. "Better get some sleep. Stop chatting with the girls and get to bed," I said.

I walked to my room shaking my head. I had to keep it together to show my students that everything was ok. My little outburst had certainly not done that. I needed sleep. I wasn't in control as much as I thought I was.

Monday night. Our second day stranded in Peru. I had a slight headache and hoped it wasn't the onset of altitude sickness. I was out of medication. I needed to be able to function and be coherent to get through the next day. With that thought, I climbed into the double bed next to Mary and set my travel alarm for four a.m.

10. Stranded: Tuesday

I woke up at four, looked outside and saw it was raining. Crap. I dressed quickly and hurried to the students' rooms to make sure they were all awake.

I had grabbed a bunch of hard rolls at breakfast the morning before and passed those out. We all quietly closed the doors to our rooms and headed down the stairs wearing our bright yellow rain ponchos, not a color that blended easily into darkness. I preferred my umbrella to the sticky plastic poncho I had purchased, but rain came down hard enough I had to wear it and use the umbrella for extra protection.

No one moved or came out to see what was going on when we closed the big glass front door and left. Matt and Julio led the way quickly down the dark street through the sleeping village. There were no streetlights, so I shined my little flashlight on the ground to keep people from tripping on rough pavement. The weak glow was almost lost in the rainy pre-dawn. The street was eerie because Aguas Calientes always seemed to be bustling.

The smell of wet smoke and soggy vegetation drifted through the mist like the remains of a campfire wafting up on a damp evening. The pleasant memory of camping helped buoy my mood. We turned a corner onto the main road and met other people bundled in rain gear heading silently in the same direction.

We arrived at the far end of the hotel where the gate to the evacuation site was located. There we joined another small group crouched against a building. I saw Phil and went over to let him know my students were ready to go. He whispered that Embassy personnel had spent the night at the landing site, but no helicopters could land yet due to the rain. I whispered to the students that we had to wait for the rain to stop.

Like us, the rest of the Americans gathered at the gate stood silently huddled together in the rain. No one checked to see if we were lined up in the order of departure decided on the bridge. The fact that we weren't told to move to the back of the line was encouraging. I wondered about the two people who had taken charge of the afternoon lottery. Where were they? I hadn't seen them at the evening meeting either.

Phil said we needed to be ready as soon as the rain lifted. The students passed that message quietly to one another. As time went on, the American group grew to around sixty individuals, all shifting from one foot to the other in the rain. I didn't recognize all of the faces. I had Hector and his family with me, and they weren't U.S. citizens. Maybe there were other non-Americans. Canadians? Germans? Maybe they'd heard about our plan and were going to sneak out with us. I wondered whether this was even the same group that had met at the bridge.

"Phil," I asked, "where are the folks who ran the lottery yesterday?"

He looked around. "Don't know. We drew numbers around two. Maybe they found another way out."

Hmm. They'd been pretty pushy setting up their system. Maybe they thought there were too many people involved and got on another helicopter? It struck me as suspicious.

No one in the soggy group looked very comfortable. Rain continued to slide off our ponchos and drip to the ground. The sidewalk was too wet to sit on, so we just stood in silence.

I began to realize that without the folks pushing their lottery system, I could just move the students along together. We needed to be patient and wait for the rain to stop. So, we waited, and we waited, and we waited, huddled close together, praying for the rain to stop.

I tried shifting my umbrella to watch the sky through the rain, but the wind whipped it inside out. The morning grew lighter, the rain continued, and the sky remained overcast. The Embassy officer on the other side of the gate regularly offered assurances that the minute the rain let up they would get the helicopters going.

During the long wait, everyone stayed quiet. Tension filled the air. Some students leaned against each other trying to sleep. Some squatted down on the sidewalk under a small overhang behind the hotel, pulling their ponchos underneath them to keep their backsides dry. After about an hour, we heard a noise below us. A group of people headed out of the village along the train tracks. About thirty minutes after that, another group entered from the opposite direction carrying what looked like a stretcher. I sucked in a deep breath. It was a body bag. Had someone died, maybe due to mudslides or drowning? The silent procession carrying their sad load unnerved me. So did watching local residents scurry away like the village was a sinking ship to be abandoned.

Some of the Americans gave up and walked back into town. I passed the word that we would continue to wait. About seven a.m., the crowd began to get restless. There was movement, someone was pushing through the group from the back. A group of local policemen elbowed their way forward.

"¡No, no pasen, váyanse! ¡No pasen!" They ordered us to leave, to go back and wait with everyone else at the main train station gate.

The students slowly began to stand up. Then Phil said, "No, no, we have permission, the U.S. Embassy is coordinating this." Phil waved for us to stay. He phoned the guy on the other side of the gate. I heard him

18. Four a.m., waiting for helicopters to arrive.

ask for someone to call up the police captain to explain what we were doing. Phil and the police passed the phone back-and-forth. The conversation ended and the officers eventually left.

Ok. That situation worked out. The police left. We just needed to wait a bit longer. The rain was slowing. The helicopters would soon be able to land. I passed my hopeful message along to the students, and they settled back down to wait.

Another thirty minutes ticked away. We heard another noise coming up from below us in the area where the train tracks led out of the city. I was shocked to see a convoy of army Jeeps pull up.

Soldiers hopped out of the vehicles carrying what looked like machine guns. The students jumped up to have a look through an opening that led to the train station. A gasp rippled through our group. An officer riding in the first Jeep stood up and stared at all of us peering down at him from the ledge. He looked like he had come from central casting for an army movie, a droopy moustache, his chest full of medals, and big epaulets on his shoulders. This guy was the real deal. He put one boot on the hood of the Jeep and shouted in a commanding voice, "*No pueden pasar. ¡Váyanse! No se permite pasar, americanos*—No going through here. Leave! You Americans may not go this way."

I called Julio over to translate. "He's saying that the Peruvian government is in charge now, not the local police or the Americans. Everyone here will need to wait their turn, there is no special treatment for anyone. I think he means us."

I looked through the opening that led down to the train tracks and could clearly see the soldiers with their guns. One of the students asked, "What do we do?"

"They have guns, so we will do exactly what they say," I replied, staring at the soldiers who seemed to be looking directly back at me.

Phil said, "I'm going to try and explain, but my Spanish is pretty limited." He raised his hand and shouted, "*Por favor,*" then started down the steps toward the soldiers.

Julio quickly chimed in, "I can translate for you." Before I could react, he was climbing down the rocky stairs with Phil.

"No editorial comments, Julio," I shouted. "Just repeat exactly what you hear." I was nervous about one of my students being so close to the soldiers, but I knew Julio could help. I just didn't want him to say anything that would get us into more trouble. I slumped back against a nearby rock wall. It was all too much. The rain, the wait, the soldiers with guns, and now Julio down there with Phil and the General having an animated conversation. I looked at Mary and mouthed, "What do you think we should do?" Mary sighed and shook her head. Neither of us had any answers.

Matt came over and asked, "What about the hotel rooms?"

"Oh my gosh, we're definitely going to need them," I replied. I explained that I'd left a deposit. Matt offered to edge out of the crowd and go back to make sure the rooms were still being held for us. He inched out behind the group and headed for the hotel.

Phil and Julio finally came back up to speak to all of us Americans. The Peruvian army had come to manage the situation. They were taking charge of the evacuation because the city and the local police weren't able to control what was happening. Julio said there were rumors that people had been bribing the Peruvian helicopter pilots to let them on the flights ahead of everyone else. Things were getting out of hand with so many people packed together in one small community. The army was sent in to restore order.

Phil added that the Peruvian army had larger helicopters that could evacuate more people on each flight. The Embassy plan to sneak us out was not going to happen. Everything would be coordinated by Peruvian army officials. We needed to follow orders.

The General had said that they would evacuate the sick first, then mothers with small children, then families with older children; then they would evacuate people in their seventies and progress downward in age, sixty and fifty-year olds and so forth. Last to go would be twenty-year-olds and older teens, of whom there were hundreds in town. Of course, that was the Gustavus students' category.

I was fifty-five, Mary sixty-two. Realistically, I knew the General would never let us leave with all the students in tow. It would be hard to make the case that we were a family. We were nevertheless responsible for the group which meant we would have to wait till the end, when they let the young adults leave.

We would just have to hunker down and wait. Matt came back and said that the hotel lobby was full of people wanting rooms, but the owner had saved ours. I was really grateful that my deposit had served its purpose. I asked Matt to go back and tell the owner that I would bring the rest of the money. I wasn't sure how I'd do this. I didn't have enough cash, and they didn't take a Visa Card. Our group of twenty-somethings got up, damp and stiff from the long wait in the rain.

Soldiers came closer and motioned with their guns. This made me nervous, but we moved along in the direction they indicated, which was toward the stadium, beyond our hotel. I hoped maybe we could all just drop out of the crowd and head into the hotel when we passed it. My anxiety rose as we kept walking right past our hotel. The students asked me what was happening, and I answered, "Just follow along, it'll be ok."

Soldiers with guns pointed in my direction was something I hadn't expected, but I was pretty sure there would be no shooting. Still, it was intimidating and scary. I tried to project a calm demeanor. When we got to the soccer stadium, the General's spokesman went over the rules. We needed to provide our names, ages and passport numbers at city hall to register for evacuation. Officials would post a departure schedule by age, so we would know our status.

After that, he said, "The people of Aguas Calientes have something for you," and a group of women brought out bread and coffee for the group. It was a lovely gesture. We sat on bleachers, drank coffee, ate rolls, and, when the sun came out, we warmed up.

19. The Peruvian Army arrives.

The town relied on tourism. I'd heard that some of the hotels were raising prices because they knew tourists were trapped and desperate. For the most part though, the residents of Aguas Calientes remained very gracious, and the simple breakfast was an example of their hospitality.

We were all exhausted, so after we ate, I suggested we check back into the hotel. Hector found me and said that he had struck out again at the ATM and was hoping I could help his family get a room. I assured him that as long as we were there, he would be a part of our group.

The owner of the hotel handed out keys and the students headed off to catch some shut eye after agreeing to meet in the lobby at noon. I just hoped we'd find a restaurant that still had food.

I looked to Mary for our room keys and saw that the owner was still holding them. Mary explained to him that I needed to withdraw cash from the ATM and would be back. There were three ATMs in town. I figured I would be able to get enough cash if I went to the two farthest from the village center.

On the way out, I ran into Javier and Cris. They offered to stand in line at two of the ATMs while I waited at the third. They strode off to hold a place in line for me, and I hit the first money machine. The banks had reduced the withdrawal maximum. I ran from ATM to ATM, hoping to get enough for the hotel bill, but with the maximum reduced, I didn't have enough to pay for our rooms.

I asked Javier, "Are there any other restaurants with cash?" hoping for another cash purchase with my credit card.

"Very few places are still open," he replied. "Restaurants that have food do not have much money on hand. And they do not take credit cards."

I went back to the hotel and asked Mary Ellen to try her card again, but it was declined. I gave the owner the money I had. He took it, counted it, and frowned. He shook his head to say it was not enough. I figured I needed to call the college and have them wire me some cash, and I asked Mary to explain this process to the owner. He wrinkled his brow. Clearly, he didn't understand how I could have money wired to his hotel. Mary assured him I would call the college and get the rest of the funds.

Finally, I put my cell phone to use. It hadn't been working very well and didn't hold a charge. I'd been communicating with Carolyn in short messages, letting her know that I would connect as I received more information, though I hadn't told her about the plan to sneak out that morning. I spied an electrical outlet behind the front desk and motioned to the owner that I wanted to use it. I crawled under the counter, plugged in my phone charger and called the college. The call went right through. I explained what had happened, that we were still in Aguas Calientes, and that I needed money wired for the cost of another might at the hotel.

"The college doesn't wire funds," she replied.

"Carolyn, I have to have some cash."

"We don't really have a system in place to do that," she answered.

"Well figure it out and get back to me. I have to have some money, or we will be sleeping on the street tonight," I shouted back into the phone. I was really upset. Wiring funds wasn't a big deal. Surely there had been situations in the past when the college had to wire money abroad. I paced around the lobby, Mary looking on and some of the students staring anxiously at me. It was hot. I felt the sweat run down my back. About five minutes later, Carolyn called back to say that the VP for finance was figuring it out, but we needed an account to wire money for payment. I handed the phone to Mary, who translated for the owner. The owner provided information and we waited. When the college called back, they said the hotel didn't have the right type of account to receive the money via a wire transfer, so they couldn't send money.

"Oh my God, this is ridiculous. There's got to be a way," I yelled into the phone.

"We need an address for somewhere in a bigger city to be able to wire the money," came the reply. "There are no wire services to receive the funds in Aguas Calientes. Ask the owner if he has contacts or relatives in Cusco or Lima where we could wire the money."

Mary translated. The owner's family owned a hotel in Cusco. He called his family and explained what would be happening, then told us we needed to wait until the money arrived. So, Mary and I waited some more. I had to lie on the floor near the outlet to make sure we didn't lose our power connection.

The sun was out. It was hot. The hotel didn't have air conditioning. The front door was propped open, but it was still sweltering. Sweat kept dripping down my back. The scent of wet vegetation wafted in from outside. Helicopters came and went with a roar about every twenty minutes to let us know that the army was at work evacuating people. Mary and Hector slumped in lobby chairs with their heads in their hands. We were all exhausted.

Then, after waiting twenty minutes, the call came in from the family that the money had arrived. The hotel owner handed over the keys to our room. I called Carolyn to let her know that the money had been transferred. She said they paid for two nights, just in case. I apologized for losing my temper, thanked her and hung up. It felt like another scene from a movie where the bank robbers are setting up overseas accounts and wiring stolen money here and there. I was amazed that we'd finally gotten everything set up. I thanked the owner once again, and Mary provided additional conversation to help smooth over what might have otherwise been a touchy situation.

I went up to the room and took a quick shower. It felt good to clean up after sitting in the rain, then sweating for so long. My clothes felt damp and smelled like mildew even after hanging in our makeshift laundry. I had nothing else to wear, so I put on the clothes I'd worn the day before.

I knew the students might be pretty discouraged by now. I certainly was. But I wanted to help keep their spirits up, so I decided to create a schedule that would give some structure to our days, since we didn't know how long we'd be stuck. If the weather held, it might not be too long, but we knew we'd be in Aguas Calientes until they evacuated all the people over the age of twenty. I found an old poster on the floor in a corner of the lobby and used the back to create a schedule:

Club Gustavus

Noon —meet in lobby for lunch

1:00—discussion of options

2:00—exploration of Aguas Calientes

3:00—card games in the lobby

4:00—planning for dinner

5:00—meet for dinner

6:30—after dinner charades with group

I knew I couldn't keep the students cooped up, but I wanted to make sure they were safe. The army had set up tents in the main Plaza for individuals from various countries, like Argentina and Chile, with additional tents for other groups. There was a lot of stuff going on out on the streets, people roaming around feeling trapped and looking for something to do. Javier said that it was pretty rowdy at night. Alcohol was still available, as well as drugs. Tempers were running high, and the potential for violence was always there.

We found a small place for lunch. With the hotel paid off, I could use the cash I got from the ATMs for meals. After lunch, I explained my poster.

"I'm not going to hold you to the schedule, but there will always be someone at the hotel for you and something to do. I insisted that we check in at mealtime and eat together. I suggested that we sit down after meals and discuss how people were feeling and talk about issues we needed to manage until we were evacuated. Back at the hotel, everyone crowded into the hot, stuffy hotel lobby.

We listened to the students' fears and frustrations. Some still had money left, and I handed out more so that they all could get water. What I hadn't known until then was that they were using their cash to access the internet café computers, which were still working. They were also spending time in line to use the only pay phone in town. Some had connected with their families. Not surprisingly, their parents were very concerned.

"How long do you think we will have to stay, until they get to us twenty-year-olds?" someone asked.

"I don't know," I replied.

"Isn't there anything else we can do?"

Brandon suggested that we email our Congressmen and Senators and have our parents do the same. "If we get our legislators on top of this, maybe they can get things moving faster. Maybe they can send more helicopters or something so we can get people out faster."

"That's a great idea," I said. "Who needs more money to use the internet?"

"It's hard to get online, there aren't many computer terminals available," said Molly.

"Still, it's good we can do something to make this situation better," I added. Then I had a major Ah-ha moment. I turned to Cris and Javier. "What about walking out? We saw people leaving this morning. Why don't we walk back to Cusco along the Inca Trail?"

Javier looked doubtful. "I don't know," he said. "It's a difficult hike."

"But these folks are young. They could do it," I replied. "Mary has a sore knee, but we can help each other."

Javier answered, "Cris and I can check it out. We will walk the trail a bit and meet you back here tonight after dinner to let you know what we find."

"Ok!" I said. I had visions of us walking across the Andes holding hands like Julie Andrews in *The Sound of Music*. Because I'd done some mountain hiking earlier in my life, I felt sure we could do it. If we hiked out, then we wouldn't have to wait for hundreds of people to leave before we got evacuated.

I suggested the students go buy water and look for a place for dinner. Jeanifer asked if they could help sandbag the rivers running through and around Aguas Caliente, all of which continued to rise rapidly. The Urbamba was the largest. The railroad ran along its banks, and it had the most water rushing through its channel.

"Of course," I replied. "You can help fill sandbags. But be careful!" Again, the Gustavus students made me proud.

The students headed off. Mary and I set up in the lobby to play cards and read. Everyone had brought a book or two, so we had a library. We swapped books and had new material to read every few days. With the front door propped open, the hotel was a bit cooler, but we still felt the heat and heard the consistent drone of the helicopters.

I carried a list with everyone's name and passport number, including Matt's. I asked him to take the list up to the army headquarters tent. He came back and reported that officials were regularly updating a poster on the wall by the post office with the ages and departure times for evacuees to move to the front of the train station.

"They've taken out the older people, sixty and seventy-year-olds. Families with children can get ready to leave later this afternoon," Matt explained.

While I was talking to Matt, Hector came up stood quietly listening. "Deb," said Hector, "Julie, Daniel and Olga can leave this afternoon. Because I am with her, and we are a family unit, I can go as well."

Hector was our go-to guy and I had relied on him, so his news stunned me. I said nothing but wondered, what I would do without him to help me think things through?

"I can go back to Cusco and get ready for when you get there with the students. You will need a hotel and new tickets to Lima."

I swallowed and nodded, feeling hollow inside.

"You'll be ok," he said. "There is really nothing more I can do for you now. I can't get money to help out, and if you do decide to walk to Cusco, I don't have experience hiking the Inca Trail. I am just a financial burden. So, I am going to check out of the hotel now, and head down to the gate."

"Ok," I gulped before giving him a long hug. "Thanks for all your help, Hector."

When Hector and his family left the hotel, I felt a wave of sadness wash over me. I looked at Mary. She shook her head, sighed and said, "We're on our own now, kiddo." We both tried to go back to reading our books, but my mind kept wandering.

I decided to call Carolyn to let her know that the sun was out. The helicopters were flying. I tried to use the phone from where I was sitting, but I needed to plug in again under the front desk. I made the call short, telling her that departures were going well, and even though Hector had left, we would manage. "As long as the sun stays out," I said, "we might be able to leave in a couple of days."

"One more thing," said Carolyn before I could hang up. "Can you keep your students off the internet? They're describing some very scary stuff to their parents and everyone around here is getting pretty upset about your situation."

"Well it is a pretty upsetting situation," I replied.

"It's just that what the students are sharing sounds very frightening to their parents," Carolyn continued. "Can you just get them to keep their conversations more positive?"

Thinking about how I might feel if I heard from one of my own children about a four-a.m. secret attempt to get out of a natural disaster area, I knew I'd be pretty upset as well. "Ok, I'll try," I said.

After the call, Mary and I wandered down to the market near the river to see what the students were up to. Kyle J. and Kevin were working side by side with local residents, sweating as they dug up dirt and filled sandbags. Both guys were tall and lanky, unlike the generally shorter and stockier Peruvians. Kyle J., who had been so shocked by the poverty when we traveled to Chimbote, was working intensely and turning pink from his time in the sun. Kevin, always cool and calm, chatted with other sandbaggers. Jeanifer was there, too, dragging the filled bags to the riverbank despite her small stature. Jeanifer's willingness to help at the river, like her empathy for the patients she saw in Chimbote, reflected her caring nature.

She had the perfect attitude for a future nurse. I smiled, proud of their volunteer efforts.

I thought about going over to help with the sandbagging, but I felt so tired. I knew stress was affecting me. I hadn't slept well, and my stomach often felt queasy. It was nice to just relax for a little bit. Mary and I sat in the shade and watched the helicopters fly in and out of the village. They came in between two mountain peaks along the Urubamba River valley, flying low over the houses and circling back to land.

20. Taking a break from sandbagging at the river.

It looked just like the opening sequence from the old *M*A*S*H** TV series. I mentioned this to Mary, who laughed and took pictures.

Aguas Calientes was an interesting place, the doorway to a World Heritage site popular with tourists from around the world. The houses were small, stacked on top of each other, climbing up the mountain behind the main streets. Most buildings were made from concrete, which kept things cool inside, and most structures did not have a finished top floor. The solid green of the tree-covered mountains could be seen from any spot in the town, and rivers dissected the community into several sections.

Up until Monday, small restaurants and little souvenir shops clustered around the bridges along the river and train tracks had bustled with activity. The local economy depended on visitors, and I wondered who was making the big money here. Who owned the upscale restaurants and hotels and the busses that took folks up to Machu Picchu? Local residents appeared to fill the jobs as salespeople, waitresses, cooks and maids. Many sold items at the market. I wondered if these were considered middle class jobs or if the economy was only a few steps up from poverty.

Later, when we all checked in back at the hotel, I asked about the students' day. Kevin talked about the sandbagging effort. He said that after sandbagging for several hours, one of the local guys went up to the restaurant and bought drinks. "He offered me a beer, but I told him 'No thanks.' I asked him where he was from, trying to get acquainted. He said, 'Argentina,' and asked me where I was from. 'We're from the U.S.'" Kevin said proudly.

Indeed, we were representing our country's good nature through the students' sandbagging work.

Kevin continued, "In return, all I got was a cold stare. The Argentinian turned around, picked up his beers and walked back to a shady spot near the restaurant's balcony. Later, I saw him pointing at us and saying something to his friends, who were now drinking the beers he'd offered me. That made me think about what other nationalities might think about us Americans here in Aguas Calientes." He paused and said, "From now on, I'm telling people I'm from Canada."

"I am proud of you for pitching in," I said. "Even if you got the brush off from the Argentinian. I'm sure you helped create a more positive image of Americans here."

"No big deal," Kevin replied.

"Still," I continued, "we have to remember that we're able to buy food and pay for the hotel. Our attempt to sneak out the other morning, and the incident with the private helicopter the first day makes us Americans look like we have privileges others don't. You need to be aware of how others might feel and just be cautious."

Other students went on to tell about their day, saying that they'd been on the internet or shopping at the craft market. "It feels like we are helping a little if we spend money here," said Molly.

Elise, one of the quieter students, spoke up. "I talked to my mom. She said there was a story about us in the paper. It's also on TV. We're famous."

There was a lot of chatter about being a news item, and everyone seemed to feel pretty upbeat. The students who'd been to the market said most of the stalls were closed, but they bought traditional drawstring pants to augment their limited wardrobes. Most of the students were already sporting colorful orange, red and green striped pants, and many wore multicolored Peruvian knit hats. The colors brightened up our rag tag group and helped us to blend in.

Cris and Javier joined us in the lobby to go to dinner. "We walked the trail for two hours," said Javier. "It will be impossible for you to do."

"Why?" I asked.

"The rain has made the trail slick, and there are a lot of mudslides. We heard that some campers were buried under the mud. People have died. The river is way up above its banks; you would have to climb pretty high up on the rocks to go over the top of the mountain, and the rocks are slippery. Even if you had equipment, ropes and good boots, it would be difficult. We know the mountains and the trails, and it was hard for us. It would be too dangerous for all of you," Javier said.

I sighed again. My vision of us walking through the mountains vanished as the reality of the danger we'd face if we tried to hike out hit me. What had I been thinking?

Javier added, "There are a lot of other guides and local people who want to follow the trail, people who have little experience. We are going to go with them and help them get to Cusco. They need all the experts they can get."

"When are you going?" I asked.

"Now. We want to make use of the daylight and sunshine," he replied.

"Ok," I said. "Take care of yourselves. We're really grateful to you for all your help. I don't know what we would have done without you." I'd come to count on Javier and Cris appearing like apparitions just when we needed help. I choked back tears at the thought of not finding them waiting to help us out anymore. I gave them each a goodbye hug.

I was really feeling abandoned. Tears were threatened to spill down my face. I took a deep breath, gave them a weak smile and watched as they ambled down the hotel stairs. I turned to the students and said that we needed to get going and hunt for a place for dinner. The students scrambled to catch up with Javier and Cris, and we walked down the street with the two guides, then watched them disappear around a corner up the road toward the mountains.

"I'm going to miss those guys," Julio said.

"Yeah," a few others echoed.

"What'll we have for dinner?" I cut in, wanting to switch things up and create a more positive mood. We would get by without our guides. We had a place to stay and money for food.

The students said that most of the places still open served exactly the same food that we had been having the past two days. Kevin, however, had found a place that also made pizza. The thought of pizza, even the greasy Peruvian version, was a big hit, and we trooped down the street energized at the thought of a good meal.

Everyone enjoyed the pizza, and after some time exchanging more stories from our day, Mary and I herded the students back to the hotel before dark. We played Celebrity, a game where we put the name of a famous person, place or thing in a hat. We divided into two groups and tried to get our teammates to guess as many of the items as possible. The first time we used words and descriptions, the second round we could only use a single word, and the last round, we pantomimed. Some were better at the game than others, getting all the clues in the minute allowed. We laughed and teased each other and enjoyed ourselves.

After the game, I suggested to the students that they hold back some on the comments they shared with their parents online. "I know you want to tell your parents what's going on," I said, "and I'm glad you can connect with them. But when you are not able to talk to someone face to face, and can only send an email, sometimes the message doesn't come out exactly how you planned. Things can be misinterpreted. People read between the lines and sense emotions that aren't there." I continued, "Your parents deserve to hear about our experience when you get home, when you're sitting next to them eating a home-cooked meal. They want to see you safe and sound. When they only read an email, or just hear your voice on the phone, all of this can seem more frightening than what's actually happening. They get the idea that you're struggling or you're not safe. You don't want to make them more worried than they already are. Try to keep your messages positive for the next few days. Your parents won't worry as much."

I saw heads slowly nod in agreement and hoped I wasn't pushing too hard. I knew some of them were homesick and close to being overwhelmed. I didn't want to cut off their connection with home. Some of them really needed to send and receive those messages. I looked around, hoping we could all keep up our spirits while we waited for our exit from Peru.

Later, I tried to get some sleep, but Mary's struggle to breathe without her C-PAP and my racing mind just wouldn't let me drift off. I felt a dull ache in my stomach, one that seemed to occur off and on since we'd been here. After a while, I took a blanket from the bed and quietly left the room to curl up on the couch in the upstairs lobby. I wasn't sure how safe it was to sleep on a sofa in a public space, but at that point, I didn't care. Finally, with thoughts of home and family in my head, I fell asleep.

11. Stranded: Wednesday Morning and Early Afternoon.

D eb ... hey, Deb. ..."

Someone tapped me on the shoulder, and I jerked awake.

"Why are you sleeping out here?" asked Alyssa. "Is anything wrong?"

I looked around. I lay on the couch with several students huddled around me.

"No, no," I answered groggily. "I just couldn't fall sleep last night, so I came out here. I thought it might be cooler." I sat up and stretched to wake myself up. My stomach growled. "Is there breakfast?" I asked.

"Yup," said Alyssa, smiling, "hard rolls and coffee!"

By some miracle, the hotel was still able to provide bread and coffee each morning. I really needed the coffee. Before breakfast, I ducked back in my room to brush my teeth. Luckily, I still had toothpaste, soap and deodorant, so I could freshen up each morning. Mary was in the shower. Still feeling somewhat beleaguered after Tuesday's events, I plugged in my cell phone and called Jon, my husband, at home. Exhausted after struggling to fall asleep late the night before, I felt I was out of ideas to keep things positive for the students. Unable to hold back tears, I let loose on Jon.

"I can't do this anymore," I wailed into the phone. I had a sinking feeling that things were not going to get better anytime soon. We could be stuck in Peru a lot longer than any of us had expected. The thought of trying to keep the students safe and constantly running out of money overwhelmed me. "I don't want to bail on the group, but I don't think I can come up with any more ideas. I don't know what else I can do to keep students from worrying." I rattled on. "I'm really trying to keep spirits up, but I'm probably not going to be able to get everyone out together. I think the group is going to get split up. If that happens, I don't know how I'll get them plane tickets or money for food. I don't want things to fall apart, but I'm not sure I am going to be able to pull this off. I just feel so fidgety and anxious. It's getting to me."

Jon listened to me rant before offering his assurance that I was up to the task. "You can do this," he said. "I know you can."

It felt good to hear Jon's voice. I'd only made one brief call to him on Sunday. His confidence in me buoyed my spirits. "Sorry I haven't been in touch," I said. "Things here have kept me busy and the phone from the college doesn't hold much of a charge."

"That's ok," said Jon. "Carolyn has been issuing press releases from the college to keep parents and the community up to date. You have other things on your mind."

"I feel like I am losing control," I sniffed. "I'm trying to keep things positive, but I'm just really tired. Sometimes, the stress makes me feel like throwing up. I don't know what to do."

"Just hang in there," he said. "You need to be strong for the students. I know you can manage this. Do that deep breathing thing you do sometimes. It'll help."

I heard Mary shut off the shower, so I quickly dried my tears. "It's just really good to hear your voice," I said. "It helps a lot."

"I love you," he said. "I'm sure I'll see you soon."

"Ok, love you, too," I replied and hung up.

I clicked off the phone and rolled off the bed. Standing barefoot on the cold floor, I took a few deep, calming breaths.

"Ok," I told myself, "time to get going on the new morning routine." After grabbing a couple of rolls and gulping a cup of coffee, I headed out to make the rounds of the three ATMS to see if I could get some cash. Luckily, the machines were still dispensing small amounts, and I was able to get enough for the day's meals. I went back to the hotel and sent students out to look for bottled water and toilet paper. I asked them to check if there was anyplace left that would take a Visa Card to pay for meals.

Chelsey Kr, looked up from writing in her journal and asked sympathetically, "Deb, how are you doing?"

That touched me. I knew the students were concerned for each other, but no one had asked about how I was doing. I smiled at Chelsey. "Ok, I guess. I'm a little tired, but I'm hanging in there."

"Good, "she replied. "I just wondered, because you really look terrible."

"Not what I was expecting, Chelsey," I laughed. "But thanks." The stress was really showing. I would have to try and relax but wondered how I was going to pull that off. I tried more slow, deep breaths, which helped a little.

Later that morning a bunch of students went out again to help sandbag. I added that to the list of the options for Camp Gustavus.

    9:00 breakfast on your own
    10:00 optional sandbagging activity at the river
    11:00 charades in the lobby
    12:00 noon—meet for check-in and lunch

21. Sandbagging teams try to hold back the raging river.

I also set up a list of days and times for everyone to choose the date we would be evacuated, kind of like a Super Bowl score betting form. Whoever came closest would get a prize. We all had different opinions on the subject. I picked Friday.

"So, what's the prize?" asked someone at breakfast.

"A burger in the Atlanta airport when we get there," I replied

"Oh yeah. I really would love a big, fat, juicy hamburger," said Josh.

As expected, with clear skies all day Tuesday, a lot of people had been airlifted out. Wednesday morning, the mist returned. The poster on the city hall door listed ages being evacuated. When age groups were announced, people headed to the train station gate. Others hoping to squeeze into groups boarding helicopters parked themselves near the station entrance.

I said to Mary, "As soon as they announce twenty-year-olds can leave, we will need to gather up the students and go sit with the crowds at the gate."

I asked Julio and Matt to check on progress. They returned to report that people in their thirties and forties were next to leave. Individuals sat and slept on the ground at the station entrance blocking access to the gate and the door. Many were twenty-year olds and not listed to leave. Still, they waited, hoping to be first in line when the twenty-year-olds were called. I wandered down to check out the situation myself. Despite all the departures on Monday and Tuesday, the train station remained crowded, which concerned me.

Mid-morning, I got word from one of the students that someone from the Embassy was in town. It turned out that a consular officer named J.J. had come to meet with Americans. I went looking for him to make sure he knew that there were still twenty-one college students and two professors in Aguas Calientes. I found J.J. talking to some Americans near the main bridge and pulled out my list of names and passport numbers. "Excuse me. I'm from Gustavus Adolphus College."

J.J. finished talking with others then turned to me with a frown. "Oh, you're that Minnesota group. Can you call off your Senators? They're making our lives miserable."

"Our Senators?"

"Yeah. They're really hot that you guys are all still here and they're flooding our Embassy with demands that we do something about the situation." J.J went on to explain that Minnesota Senators Amy Klobuchar and Al Franken, and First District Congressman Tim Waltz were inundated by calls from the students' parents and friends. So, in turn, the legislators were pushing for the State Department to get us out.

I thought to myself with a smile, "Maybe something is going to happen."

J.J. continued. "Minnesota, right?"

Then, Sara, the Embassy official I had talked to on the phone earlier in the week, joined us. I handed her my list of names and passport numbers. Sara smiled and said, "We're working on getting everyone out." Her tone was pretty non-committal as far as reassurances go. I headed back to the hotel to let Mary and the students know the impact of their efforts to get our legislators involved.

"Yes!" exclaimed Brandon with a fist-pump, "the power of the people to get government moving." I quietly hoped Brandon wouldn't be too disillusioned if the government was unable to speed up our evacuation.

We went to lunch as a group and discovered that restaurants still open wouldn't take credit cards, so I used cash I had gathered that morning. After lunch, several of the guys headed off to buy sandals. In the wet, humid atmosphere, their shoes were hopelessly soggy and unbelievably stinky. Allyssa and Alison went over to a home laundry we'd seen on our way to lunch. They wanted to get their clothes cleaner than we were able to do in the sink.

"I am tired of my clothes smelling," complained Alyssa. "Besides, the clothes we hang up on the roof never really get dry, just less damp."

I understood. I'd put on damp underwear that morning, though I felt better because they at least seemed clean.

The rest of group drifted back to the hotel lobby and started another game of Celebrity, which we were playing when J.J. walked into the room.

"I brought you some apples," he said by way of introduction. It was a weird way to make an entrance, tossing us apples, but we caught them, laughed and began munching. We hadn't eaten much fresh fruit and enjoyed the treat.

J.J. watched us enjoying the apples and the game. He spotted our exit prediction chart and asked, "Can I add my bet?

"Sure," I said.

He wrote something then he turned the paper for us to read. "Wednesday, three-thirty."

Students squealed with excitement and peppered J.J. with questions.

"You can get us out?"

"We're leaving now?"

"How's this going to work?"

I interrupted to ask, "How do you know we can leave now?"

"Peruvian officials will be calling for twenty-year-olds later this afternoon. Your group is so big, we're going to have you guys leave first." The students cheered. J.J. continued, "Get packed. You have to get going."

Everyone ran off to grab their stuff, laughing with excitement. There were four students out in the village. I had to get word to them, but I didn't want to make a big deal of it. I sent the first students who came down with their bags to go get the girls at the laundry.

"Anyone know where Josh went to get sandals?" I asked. No one seemed to know, so I left a note telling them to pack and meet us at the train station gate. About then, Alyssa and Allison hurried into the lobby. "Where's your laundry?"

"We left it. It wasn't done. The laundry lady can keep our clothes. We just want to go home," said Alyssa.

Then Josh ran up behind me. "Hey, what's going on?" He looked around and saw everyone had their backpacks loaded up. "Deb, were you going without us? You said we'd all go together."

"I left a note so you would know where to find us," I responded.

Josh looked at me with indignation and maybe a little fear. "You were leaving without us."

"No, I would never leave without you," I reassured him. "But we had to get organized and down to the train station. We wouldn't have left without you."

Staying together had become ingrained in all of us. The intensity of our connectedness was so strong that even six-foot-tall Josh got a little frantic at the thought of being left behind. His reaction made it clear to me that we were all suffering a bit of trauma from our situation. I hoped that J.J.'s information was accurate. We didn't need to be disappointed again. We needed to go home.

The students hustled down to the train station and J.J. had us sit on the edge of a cement border above and around the corner from gathering crowds. Word had gotten out that twenty-year olds were leaving and several hundred young people jammed in around the gate. J.J. and Sara went to check out the situation.

Soldiers guarded the doorway through the gate into the main train station. Upriver, we could see the helicopters setting down on the bank behind the gated area where we'd waited on Tuesday morning. Sitting there waiting in the sun was an uneasy reminder of what we'd already been through.

J.J. came back and told us that the Embassy had coordinated with the army. They agreed to take our group out first. "We're going to go into the station in just a few minutes," he said.

I looked down at the number of people milling around by the entrance. Every time the guards opened the door, several people pushed forward and rushed through. There was definitely some shoving going on as people pressed toward the entrance.

I looked at J.J. "It's intense down there," I said. "Maybe we should wait until the crowd is smaller."

"Nope," he said, "We're doing this." J.J. turned to the students. "Ok, here we go. Have your passport in hand so they can look at it as you go through. Sara will go first. The rest of you follow her. I'll bring up the rear. Just move quickly."

I looked at the students sweating in the hot sun. They could see and hear the crowd and I knew they suspected the exit might be a little rough.

"All right," I said. "Keep your passport in hand but close to your body. And keep your head down. Don't look at anyone, don't say anything. This is J.J.'s plan, but not everyone down there may be ok with us leaving first. Just be cool and keep walking. Lock arms if necessary. Stay close behind the person in front of you. Try to avoid gaps in our line."

We organized ourselves single file. I would lead. Mary would go last ahead of J.J. "Let's go," I said.

Chelsea Ko took a deep breath and shook her head. "I can't walk through that mob," she said, her voice shaky, close to tears.

"Come up here next to me," I said. "We'll be through the crowd in no time." I took her by the arm, trying hard to push down my own growing fear. I pasted a smile on my face, nodded to the students and gave a thumbs-up.

Sara led the group single file down through the market and around the corner. She moved more quickly as we started through the crowd. It felt like the parting of the Red Sea. Speaking loudly in Spanish, Sara elbowed her way through to the gate. Young people also trying to get out closed in on our right and left. There were a lot of angry faces and we heard some pretty intense voices. I wondered if the crowd would let us through.

We stood there for what seemed like an hour. In reality, only a few minutes passed. We were obviously a group of Americans. Insults were being hurled at us. Then the soldiers shouted something and began opening the door. The crowd surged forward.

Sara started through the gate. I tightened my grip on Chelsea Ko's arm and followed. The crowd pressed in against us. There was a brief pause. The crowd grew louder. The gate opened wider. Everybody saw what was happening. The Americans were going first.

"¡No! ¡No pasen!" yelled the crowd, shoving us roughly through the opening. Others, not our students, pushed us aside and ran ahead. I stumbled through the gate, linked with Chelsea, Mary Ellen and Elise, nearly falling from the momentum.

Suddenly, the guards slammed the heavy gate shut behind us. They shouted, "No mas, no mas!" People crowded against the fence on the other side. I ran up to the gate on my side and began pleading with the soldiers.

"¡Mis estudiantes! ¡Es importante los estudiantes venga conmigo!—My students! It is important that my students come with me." I shouted in broken Spanish. "Yo tengo las ticketas para todas las estudiantes y todo el dinero.—I have the tickets for all the students and all their money."

Voices hollered back in English and Spanish, "If you have a

ticket, let me through. I'll be your student!"

"I'm a student of life. Let me come with you."

"You don't get to go first!"

"You Americans, stop using your money to buy your way out!"

Jeers echoed across the station in English, Spanish and a few other languages I didn't recognize. I couldn't understand everything, but I understood the tone. People were mad. Pushing on the other side of the gate intensified. The Gustavus students stood mutely, eyes down. The crowd continued to squeeze in around them. J.J. walked alongside my students trying to calm the mob while subtly pushing the encroaching people back.

"Mi otra profesora esta enferma," I cried, motioning for Mary to come to the gate. I thought if I could get Mary through by telling the guards that she was sick, the rest of the students could follow.

The Peruvian general stood nearby observing the situation. He yelled in Spanish to the crowd, "Those American students have to go. Their leaders are old. They need to leave."

J.J. walked Mary, limping, to the gate. Soldiers opened the door. She hobbled forward. I think because it was clear that Mary was older than all the other people in the crowd, they let her pass without hassle. I rushed over and helped her to a nearby bench. "Play it up!" I whispered, "make it seem like you are really hurting."

Mary nodded and began rubbing her leg. She spoke to the crowd in Spanish "All the students need to go with us because we have a group ticket." She pointed at me. "We're old. We needed to leave. I hurt my knee," she said, rubbing it and moaning. At that moment, Mary deserved an academy award, though in reality, she was not doing well.

There were more cries of dissent from the crowd. I went back to the gate and pleaded with the crowd to let my students through. Sara came over and told me to get away from the gate.

"You're making things worse," she said, and led me by the arm away from the opening. "You need to back down. Stop antagonizing the crowd."

I was taken aback. Me? Antagonizing? I didn't think that was what I was doing. I looked at Sara, distraught, but complied. Mary limped over to a shaded bench. We sat down with the three girls who had made it through the gate.

Sara gave me a tight smile. "Just relax. This is not a big deal. I've done a lot of extractions. When you get home, this will just be another interesting story to tell."

"Extraction?" I had visions of an army operation with strategists working behind the scenes. "This is not a little thing to us, Sara. This is a big deal," I replied.

"It happens a lot," Sara went on, "people get a little vocal, a little pushy. Everything'll work out fine. We're going to call the security people and figure this out."

Sara phoned somebody back by the helicopters then waved to a man running in our direction. I got even more nervous when I saw he was dressed all in black with "U.S. Military" printed on his shirt. He looked like he belonged on a SWAT team. He was on his phone as well. I heard him say, "So you want me to bring the rest of the American college group? You sure? I'm telling you, we're close to a riot out there."

Oh, no. Not a riot. I ran over to Sara. "We don't need to go right now," I said emphatically. "We can wait. I'll go back through the gate and we'll wait until the last person leaves if we need to. I don't want there to be a riot. I just want to keep my students safe." Feeling panicky, I repeated, "We'll just walk back out and wait until things calm down."

Sara turned away. I grabbed her arm and pleaded, "We'll just go back to the hotel."

Sara waved me off and got back on her phone. A few minutes later, the General, his hat cocked at a perfect angle, stalked over. He began issuing loud orders to his soldiers. Sara turned to me and said, "Your students will be ok. Just a few more minutes. We've started this and we need to finish it. I'll get you all through." She walked over and spoke with the General in rapid Spanish.

After their conversation, the General got on his phone. Soon, a half dozen more Peruvian soldiers ran up on the other side of the gate, formed a line on either side of my students and began easing the crowd back. The angry crowd facing the military pushed back. It looked scary. Mary translated for me. "The General's strategy is for his soldiers to let a few tourists through followed by a few of our students, followed by more tourists, then more from our group."

The General spoke to the crowd in a strong, official voice. His plan was to equalize numbers leaving from each group.

Hoping the process would calm things down, I jogged back to the other side of the train station where the three girls and Mary waited. I had not run at that altitude wearing my backpack. By the time I reached Mary, I struggled to breathe, bent over, wheezing and gasping, unable to talk.

"Oh my god, what is it?" asked Chelsey Ko. "What happened?"

I shook my head, continuing to gasp. "I can't run in this altitude," I said. The girls laughed with relief. I'd scared them. They thought something horrible had happened. "No," I said between gasps, "I just wanted to remind you to wait for the rest of us. Even if they ask you to move on, wait. We all go together."

"We definitely don't want to go by ourselves," Chelsey Ko. assured me.

I walked back to the entrance taking slow, deep breaths to calm my racing heart for fear that I would pass out. When I got there, the gate opened. About ten young people squeezed through and ran off to the other side of the train station. The gate slammed shut. There was a pause. Then a soldier, responding to a signal from the General, motioned the Gustavus students through. As soon as the soldiers began to open the gate, the restless crowd shouted, *"¡No! ¡No pasen!"* and pressed against my students.

Sara motioned the students through. "Quickly, move quickly please."

My stomach tied itself into a knot. About six students stumbled through, ran over to me and collapsed. I gave them each a big hug. The crowd continued yelling at the students on the other side of the gate. I asked Molly if she could translate. Molly said she asked Julio that very question. "Julio told me, 'You don't want to know.'"

At this point, the crowd merged into one big mass straining to get to the gate. It was hard to see my students. I'd never had an ulcer, but right then I worried I might develop one.

Time passed. The gate opened and a few more stranded young tourists squeezed through. The gate slammed shut again. I scanned the mob to locate my students. The gate suddenly opened and the remainder of the Gustavus students burst through the opening followed by J.J. I ran over as they scrambled through the doorway.

"Thank God," I cried, trying to hug them all. "Is everybody ok?"

"My passport!" Kyle J. gasped, looking around frantically. "My passport got knocked out of my hand when we were going through the gate."

Allison, who had come through behind Kyle, waved his passport in his face. "I saw it fall and scooped it up," she said. Kyle grinned and hugged her.

"Way to go," I said, laughing shakily. I counted to make sure everyone was there. The gate clanged shut. Shouting intensified.

Kevin, who had been at the back of the line, had his arms around Katie, practically dragging her.

"Did she faint?" I asked.

"No, she got shoved out of line and into the crowd," he said. "She needed some help."

"Somebody knocked me down. I thought I was going to get trampled!" Katie gasped. "Kevin grabbed me and pulled me through the gate."

"Are you ok?" I asked.

Tears brimming in her eyes, Katie nodded, "Yes."

"Kevin, you're awesome," I said, hugging him.

I breathed a great sigh of relief that the students had been looking after each other. Our tight group connection amazed me.

Sara came over and said, "You need to knock off the hugging and get moving. J.J. and I are going back to help more young people through. We can meet up later, Deb. Good luck."

"Thanks. I don't know what to say."

"No need to say anything," said J.J., waving me off. "You need to get moving."

We turned and jogged down the sidewalk beside parked train cars. Peruvian soldiers directed us to step inside one of the rail cars serving as a staging area. We would have to wait a while longer for departure. A solider handed out packaged sandwiches and bottles of water. We sat there, relieved in spite of the palpable tension in the air. "What next?" I wondered. Every now and then a soldier would appear, count off a group, and wave them forward.

"Hey, you guys," I said to the students. "Remember what I said about staying together. We may get separated in the helicopters, but we will all end up in the same place, so stick together. No one left behind. If it looks like you'll be separated from the group, or that you'll be left alone, step back, let somebody else go. Be sure they're at least two of you."

Sitting together inside the train car, I had a chance to unwind, relax, and realize that we were all finally heading out of Aguas Calientes. In a day or two we would be home. After about twenty minutes, a soldier stuck his head in our car and motioned for us to move out.

Soldiers pointed toward a path behind the hotel, above the train tracks, through the jungle. "*Rápido, rápido, rápido.*"

I felt like we were caught in another old movie, jogging along a path through a swath of jungle, vines dangling overhead, the smell of earthy vegeta-

22. Helicopters arrive.

tion and mud all around us. Through gaps in the trees, I could see we were following the riverbank. At the sound of a helicopter coming in, we stopped and watched our rescuers descend from the sky and come in low between two mountain peaks and land by the river. Another M*A*S*H* moment. Images of old American movies and television seemed to color my impressions of the experience.

The roar of the helicopters overhead intensified. We were close. The line of people ahead of us stopped. Suddenly everything grew quiet. We could hear the whoosh of helicopter blades slowing, birds squawking and the rush of the river.

"How's this all going to work?" Brandon asked, looking around at the line-up of Gustavus students.

I could see by the look on their faces that most of the students were wondering the same thing. I strolled down the line calmly and reminded them that we were almost out of Aguas Calientes.

Mary told me she'd heard the soldiers say that the helicopters were taking the evacuees back to Ollantaytambo, south-west of our location and site of the Sun Temple we had visited days before. The road from Ollantaytambo to Cusco was passable. Busses would take us the rest of the way.

"We'll reconnect when we get to the village," I said. "Everybody wait for all of us to arrive. We'll probably be put onto different helicopters." I looked down the path to make sure the students were listening. "Got it?" I asked. They nodded and gave me a thumbs-up. I continued, "Whatever you do, when you board the helicopter, don't get on alone. Make sure you're with at least one other person from our group. Just step back and let someone else go before you if you need to. Make sure no one from our group is left alone and we'll rendezvous later."

A stream of men suddenly marched toward us from the helicopter landing area carrying cases of water and large bags of rice and beans, supplies for local residents. We stepped back against the foliage to let the sweating men pass. They rushed by hauling large bags through the humid jungle on their backs or balanced on their heads. I was glad that the village was getting supplies, and I was glad that we were finally leaving.

12. Evacuation: Late Afternoon, Wednesday

O ur departure was not as quick as we thought it would be. When J.J. came into our hotel lobby earlier, tossing apples and looking like a special agent with his sunglasses and cargo vest, he made it sound like we would be quickly whisked out of Aguas Calientes. But there was a process in place that meant more waiting. I noticed Gustavus students standing around in several different small groups. The gatekeepers had let other tourists through between our students. We weren't grouped together, which made keeping an eye on everyone difficult.

The wait was excruciating. My former student Matt had taken on the role of Mary's assistant, helping her along the rough path and ensuring she didn't stumble and make her sore knee worse. Mary, Matt and I formed the last group of Gusties inching forward. Stopping. Inching forward. Stopping. Again and again. The heat and humidity were awful. Sweat trickled down my back even when we stood motionless. I distracted myself by swatting at gnats flying around my head and shifting from foot to foot. I knew we were close to getting out, but I was anxious and wanted to keep moving.

We were in an area behind the hotel on a path created as a nature walk for hotel patrons. A cage with tropical birds sat by the side of the trail. Hanging placards indicated the names of plants and trees. It felt odd to be experiencing a beautiful jungle walk while waiting anxiously for extraction. At one point, Brandon held a leaf in his hand, examined it and said, "Nice fern!" We all smiled at the irony of the resort location.

Slowly moving forward finally positioned us where we had a view of the choppers through the trees. Helicopters were landing in two locations. Large military choppers set down on a wide grassy area near the river. Smaller helicopters landed behind us on a slight slope.

23. Evacuation.

Soldiers continued to walk down the line counting off groups of people and sending them forward to board helicopters in one of the two landing spots. The big military helicopters looked like they held about twenty individuals. People ran forward from the trail, stopped and crouched down in the tall grass below the whirring blades. They huddled in a tight line, waiting for a signal.

Military personnel offloaded supplies to the porters. The unloading and boarding happened quickly. We watched evacuees haul themselves onboard. Some helped people struggling to get on. Choppers came in, supplies were removed, passengers got on, then the helicopter roared off over the village, circling back over our heads on the way to Ollantaytambo. Behind us, groups of six scrambled up the hill to board the smaller helicopters. I assumed these were the choppers the State Department told us about on the aborted early morning evacuation attempt. I relaxed and slowly inched forward, glad that I had instructed the students to stay together.

Mary pointed out a large group of our students hunched down in the grass waiting for a military helicopter. Sarah H, who was constantly snapping photos, squatted at the front of the line leaning back to get a good shot of an incoming helicopter. She fell backwards onto the person behind her, knocking everyone into each other like a line of falling dominos. They all ended up on their butts in the dirt.

I found it hilarious and laughed at all of them sprawled on the ground, their heavy backpacks making it hard to turn over and get up. The soldiers laughed as well but urged the group to hurry. The group rolled around and flipped back over into a squat before hustling onto the helicopter.

The rest of our students had moved close to the departure area. I shifted my weight back and forth and tried to relax. I had a slight headache, probably not altitude sickness. I was really tired and achy. The sky gradually changed while I watched. Clouds moved in and a slight mist fell.

I thought, "Don't start raining now. We have to get everyone out today." I felt incredibly frustrated and began praying silently, "Please, God, don't let the rain keep us from leaving today." I repeated the same prayer over and over as the rain intensified.

When I saw the last of our students run forward to board a helicopter, Mary, Matt and I shuffled forward a few steps. I'd wanted to keep an eye on the students, so I intentionally stayed behind. A solider walked up to us, counted off six people with his rifle and directed us up the small hill. We were leaving!

There was not a trail, so Matt and I helped Mary. We scrambled up a rocky outcrop. The plateau at the top was a driving range, a part of a golf course or a practice area for golfers staying at the resort hotel. It was funny seeing an area associated with lavish vacation activity turned into a helicopter landing pad.

Our group of six squatted when the next helicopter landed, crouching under whirling blades blowing around manicured grass and shrubs. The gusts created by the chopper were powerful. My hair whipped in my face and my clothing flapped.

When the chopper touched down, one of the soldiers motioned for us to board. They kept glancing up at the sky. It was clear they were worried about the rain as well. "¡Rápido, rápido!" they shouted. Our group moved ahead, Mary, Matt and I were the second, third and fourth in line.

The first person climbed aboard our helicopter. Matt moved forward to help Mary on board. Last in our small queue were two Canadian teenagers chattering anxiously in English. I had talked to both girls earlier. All of a sudden one of the soldiers stopped behind me and put up his hand. "Alto!" he shouted, motioning for me and the girl behind me to move forward. Then he put up his hand, stopping the last girl in line.

"¡No más!" he said, motioning for me and the girl behind me to board but preventing the last person, the second Canadian teen, from boarding.

"No!" The girl wailed, realizing she was not getting on the helicopter with the rest of us. "Don't leave me! You can't leave me," she cried, her voice shrill with hysteria. She lurched forward to grab at her friend, but the soldier put up his hands, motioning her to back up. The first person to board had been a large, heavy individual, which was probably why the helicopter could only take five people instead of six.

The Canadian girl behind me held her companion's arm. "You can wait with me for the next helicopter." The other girl tried to pull away, but her friend clung to her arm, pleading for her not to leave. She sobbed and grabbed hold of her friend's shirt, but the girl pulled away and ran past me, hunched down, to board the helicopter.

"¡Una más!" the soldier hollered, holding up one finger and then waving for me to get moving. I took a couple steps forward, crouching, then turned around to look at the hysterical young Canadian behind me.

The girl cried out, "Please, don't leave me!" She looked frantic with the wind whipping her hair, and tears streaming down her face.

The image of my daughter Laura flashed through my mind. This girl looked to be about the same age, and her sobs tore at my heart. What if it was Laura in this situation? Or one of my own students? The thought of leaving this scared young person all alone was not something I could do. In an instant of well-intended sympathy, I waved her onto the helicopter ahead of me.

She gasped, then quickly ran past me sobbing, "Thank you, thank you, thank you."

I crouched down low again to watch the girl scramble up into the helicopter. The door slammed shut and the chopper swiftly rose into the mist that had begun to thicken. I felt big drops splash onto my face as the helicopter disappeared into the gray sky.

"Well, crap," I exclaimed as the rain began in earnest. "What the hell did I just do?"

I'd made a spur of the moment decision, thinking I'd just get on the next helicopter and all would be good. But with thick raindrops pelting my face, I knew I had messed up big time. Despite all my admonitions to the students, I had managed to get myself left behind. Rain fell harder. A soldier motioned me back down the hill. I knew I was not leaving that day. I'd violated the one big rule I'd constantly preached to my students.

I collapsed on a boulder and wondered what to do next. I'd failed to get us all out together. Tears welled up in my eyes. My body began to tense up at the thought of heading back through the crowd at the train station. I would need to find a place for the night. If I couldn't find a hotel with a vacancy, I might have to sleep outside, the price for screwing up.

Suddenly there was a loud roar. A soldier headed down the hill turned back. A much smaller helicopter with a glass bubble front hovered over the hill and started to land. *"¡Tres personas! ¡Tres más!*— Three people, three more," yelled the soldier. In a few seconds, three young men scrambled up, followed by the soldier. He motioned me and the three men to squat down, then ran over to the helicopter door, opened it, had a quick word with the pilot, and waved us on board. The rain and wind were intense, but in a matter of seconds the helicopter took off, up into the rain and clouds, roaring over the village, circling to gain altitude and rising above the mountains. I collapsed back into my seat, amazed that I was airborne.

"This is so cool!" one of the young men shouted above the roar of the helicopter. His friends nodded and they high fived each other.

"Where're you from?" I asked

"California," they responded. "We didn't see this type of helicopter before. The others had small windows, but this bird has glass all around. Look at that view!"

I glanced down, amazed at the scene of the village receding behind us as we sped through the gap between the mountains. The rain continued and the helicopter was buffeted about, causing several drops in altitude that left my stomach in my throat.

"Awesome!" the boys cried as we bounced up and down. "Look, you can see for miles."

Just then, the pilot turned around. He actually took his hands off the steering device to lean backward over his seat. I thought that his co-pilot must be flying the chopper, but I wasn't sure. I gasped.

The pilot smiled and said something, waving his hands for emphasis. Then he turned back around and took over steering.

"What? What did he say?" I asked my companions.

"He said that he didn't have enough fuel to land this helicopter and depart again in the rain. He's not going to go to Ollantaytambo. We're going directly to Cusco."

"Cool!" another of the boys cried. "We get to miss the bus ride to Cusco!"

Dread filled me. My stomach lurched. I was not going where all my students were.

"*¡No, no!*" I cried, tapping the pilot on the shoulder. "*Mis estudiantes estan en Ollantaytambo. Es necesito yo voy a la Ollantaytambo, no Cusco.*—My students are in Ollantaytambo, I need to go there, not to Cusco."

"*No es posible,*" The pilot yelled back at me.

"Not possible," one of the guys echoed, grinning at me.

"Just relax. No one else is getting the grand tour of the Sacred Valley," said another. They proceeded to point out some of the Inca sites visible through the rain and clouds.

"Ahhgg!" I though. "Another screw up! How will I get a hold of Mary and my students? How will they know where I am?" Mary was probably confused about why I hadn't boarded with them. "How could this happen?"

I took a quick peek out the window and had to admit that the view was stunning. The sight of the misty Andes was impressive. Craggy mountain tops stood in the distance. The river valley curved below. I felt like I was in the middle of an IMAX movie with all the stomach dropping thrills.

I'd never been in a helicopter. The ride was scary and exciting, but I couldn't enjoy it. My mind was busy trying to figure out how to connect with Mary once I got to Cusco. I had the plane ticket vouchers and all the money; I carried our only phone. "I'll have to figure out how to call her." Mary would wait for me in Ollantaytambo and keep the students with her while she tried to figure out where I was. My stomach roiled from the flight as well as my anxiety and fear. I wracked my brain trying to decide what to do.

I'd need to find somewhere to plug in the phone, and hopefully it would work. It didn't always connect to the number I dialed. Using it was frustrating, but necessary.

Mary should have had another phone similar to mine. She left it at home, which hadn't seemed like a big deal until now. Things wouldn't seem so unmanageable if she had a phone.

We landed on the tarmac at the Cusco Airport, a long way from the terminal building. I ran across the blacktop and hustled inside to look for someone to help me. If I could find out where the helicopters were landing in Ollantaytambo, I could get someone to help me make a call. As soon as I entered the airport, I was herded into a line facing a table with several harried administrative types holding clipboards. They pointed to a page where I needed to write down my name and passport number. I scribbled the information, then asked for help.

"¿Ayúdame, por favor? Dónde estan las otras personas de Ollantaytambo?—Help me please? Where are the other people from Ollantaytambo?" I got no response. "¡Por favor! Mis estudiantes estan en Ollantaytambo, yo estoy aqui. ¡Es un problema!—Please! My students are in Ollantaytambo and I am here. It's a problem!"

One of the women finally noticed my concern and looked up from what she was doing. "¿Qué es el problema?—What is your problem?" she asked, adding several other sentences in rapid Spanish. She seemed to understand me, but I had no idea what she said.

"Es importante yo teléfono a mis estudiantes en Ollantaytambo—It is important that I telephone my students in Ollantaytambo," I said. She shook her head and waved me on, so I stepped aside to let others sign in. My Spanish dictionary was in my bag at the hotel. I looked around and noticed that the three young men with me on the helicopter had signed in and left. Frustrated, I struggled with what to do next, when suddenly one of the guys from the helicopter came back.

"Hey," he said, "are you looking for a group of college students from Minnesota?"

"What?" I stammered. "Yes, yes. I'm trying to find out where they are."

"Well, there's a group over by the door," he replied. "I told them somebody back here is freaking out looking for them."

"Oh my god, thank you." I followed him out of the entry area. Just then my phone buzzed.

"Hello?" I said, hoping it was Mary. It was my son, Matt.

"Hi, Mom," he said. "Dad said you might appreciate a call. How are you doing?"

My son was calling to support me, but I was too stressed out to talk. "Matt," I said, "I love that you're calling to cheer me up. Right now, I need to find my students. I just arrived in Cusco and I think they're somewhere in this airport. I've got to go see what's up. Can I call you back later?"

"Sure," Matt replied, "I just wanted you to know I was thinking about you."

"Thanks, honey," I said. "I'll call you later. Love you." I felt terrible. It was so sweet of him to call, but I couldn't concentrate on a conversation with Matt when I didn't know where my students were.

Around the corner in the main terminal, I spied a group of eight Gustavus students sitting huddled together. I hurried over to them.

"Deb!" they yelled. "Thank god you're here. We figured someone from our group would end up here eventually. We didn't know what to do so we just found a place to sit and chill. This is where they're bringing everybody, isn't' it?"

"No," I responded, giving each of them a hug. "Most of the helicopters are taking people to the village of Ollantaytambo. They'll be bussed the rest of the way to Cusco. How did you end up here?"

"Our pilot seemed to be at the end of his shift or something," one of the students said. "He got out after we did and headed into the hanger."

"Where is everybody else?"

"Are we heading home today?"

"Is Hector meeting us?"

Their questions kept coming, none of which I could answer.

"I don't know about the rest of the students. I think I got on the last helicopter out of Aguas Calientes before it started raining again," I said.

Someone asked, "Do you think Mary will get on a bus without all of us being together?"

"I don't know," I replied. "Mary isn't one to mess around. I think she'll wait there for the rest of us, at least for a while. I need to call the bus station or wherever they are and try and get ahold of her."

Nicole and Sara B, who definitely had better Spanish than me, pointed out an information booth. We headed over to try to connect with Mary. Nicole explained our predicament and asked for the number of the bus station in Ollantaytambo. The woman in the booth gave me a number to call.

When I tried calling, my cell phone died after a few seconds. "I need a place to plug in the phone," I said.

The students scrambled around and found an outlet. I plugged in and called the number again. The person who answered couldn't understand me, so I handed Sara B. the phone and she explained our situation. Turned out, we hadn't called the bus station.

Just then, a man in a uniform came over and asked in halting English if he could help. I explained again. He tried to call the number I'd been given on his cell phone then shook his head. "No luck," he said. He went over to the information booth and asked for help. The person working there tried calling another number. No answer.

Eight tired and hungry students sagged back down to the floor. I pocketed my worthless phone. "Let's go to the hotel Hector arranged for us," I said. Hotel Ruinas, where we'd stayed earlier, was our destination. I looked around for a couple of taxis to get us there, then searched my bag to see if I had enough cash to pay for the ride.

"Let me help," offered the man in uniform. He went to the door and whistled. A station wagon pulled up. "I'll have my driver take you to your hotel."

I was not functioning on all cylinders or I would have questioned whether it was safe to get into a car, especially, a car that was not a taxi, with somebody we didn't know. But I didn't have enough money for a cab, so I agreed. I assured the students that I would continue to try to find Mary from the hotel. "It's time to leave the airport and get some food," I said.

We piled into the station wagon. The uniformed man jumped in as well. He told me he was an airport official and happy to help us get to our hotel. I was so glad to have someone else in charge, that I never gave it another thought. Reflecting on it later, I know we were lucky that he was, indeed, another helpful Peruvian official. He delivered us to the Hotel Ruinas. We thanked him and headed to the door. The man waved as the car drove off. I never did get his name.

Hector, who heard the commotion when we arrived, hustled out to greet us. "I told you to call and I would come get you at the airport," Hector admonished.

"It was just too crazy," I replied, "and, of course, my phone died."

"Come on, let's get you settled," said Hector. "The owner of the hotel heard about what happened. She is providing dinner for all of you."

"That's awesome," I said with a smile. The students cheered and went to retrieve their stored bags, pick up room keys and drag luggage to their rooms.

Hector looked around and asked, "Where is Mary? And where are the other students?"

I explained what happened. "Can you contact the bus station in Ollantaytambo," I asked?

"I'll try."

We sat in the front lobby of the hotel while Hector called information then tried to reach the bus station in Ollantaytambo. When he finally connected with someone, he asked several questions in rapid-fire Spanish. After a few minutes, he turned to me and shook his head. "They say the helicopters stopped landing after the rain started. There is no one waiting at the station. The last bus to Cusco left just a little bit ago."

"Can you ask who was on that bus? Describe Mary," I said. "There should be thirteen students with her."

Hector related the information. After a minute, he shook his head again. "The lady on the phone said the bus station is closing for the day. She couldn't see the busses from her office. She doesn't know who was on them."

He looked me in the eyes and said confidently, "I am sure Mary and the students got on a bus and will be here soon."

"You don't know Mary," I replied. "She's determined. She'll wait for me. When I didn't get on the helicopter with her, she probably thought I'd come on the next one." I thought about it for a minute. "Maybe she took the students somewhere else to wait," I said.

"Maybe," Hector answered doubtfully.

"This has been a hell of a day," I said, feeling discouraged. "Hector," I continued, "I've lost thirteen college students and my colleague. Counting Matt, that's fifteen people. I don't think I've ever had a worse day in my life. I've never felt so many emotional highs and lows in such a short time."

I trudged over and got my room key, my stored bag, and schlepped my suitcase up the stairs. "Oh, for an elevator," I thought. I used my remaining strength to pull the large bag up the stairs. I fumbled to get my key in the lock. Just then my phone rang again, and I thought it might be my son Matt.

"Hello?"

"Is this Deb Pitton," a voice asked?

"Yes, who's this?" I said.

"I am calling from the Center for International and Cultural Education at Gustavus. I got a call from Mary Solberg."

"Just a minute, I have to plug in before I lose you," I interrupted, quickly shoving my phone charger into a nearby wall socket. "Hello? Hello?" I yelled into the phone.

"I have a message from Mary Solberg to pass on to you."

"Oh my God!" I cried. "What did Mary say? Where is she?"

"She said to tell you that she and fourteen students are on a bus heading for the Cusco airport. She hopes you will be able to have someone pick them up."

"Can you call her back?" I asked.

"I can try."

"Tell her that Hector will pick them up. We're at the Hotel Ruinas waiting for them."

"Ok."

I clicked off my phone and let out a huge sigh of relief before hollering down the stairs to tell Hector about the call.

"I have a bus ready to go," he said. "How did you get the call?"

"Mary must have borrowed someone's phone and called the Gustavus International Center. That's how I got the message."

"We all made it, Deb," said Hector, grinning.

"We sure did!" I laughed; a huge weight suddenly lifted off my shoulders.

Hector left to pick up the rest of the crew. I headed to my room and immediately took a shower. The steamy water felt great. I stood under the spray for at least a half hour, letting the dirt and sweat and stress of the past four days wash away. I put on the last of my clean clothes and headed downstairs to the dining room.

The students milled around drinking Coca tea, waiting for dinner. They had also cleaned up. They'd put away their Inca clothing and wore jeans and t-shirts. The hotel owner came in to offer condolences for our experience, and to tell us the servers would be bringing our dinner out in a few minutes.

"Can we wait a bit longer until the rest of the students get here?" I asked.

"We will bring you food, and keep some warm for everyone else," she said. I think she could see the hungry look in my students' eyes. The last thing we'd eaten were the packaged sandwiches in the train station in Aguas Calientes.

We pushed smaller tables around to form a big table and all sat together, including seats for the missing group members. We were passing the bread and soup was being served when we heard a loud commotion at the main door. Suddenly, thirteen students, plus Matt and Mary, burst through the door. We all jumped up, cheered, and ran to hug each other. The noisy reunion continued as we clambered into chairs to eat dinner.

Mary wearily lowered herself into the seat next to me. "What happened to you?" she demanded.

I explained about the girl who was about to be left behind, and she shook her head. "I thought you'd been hurt or something," she said. "You were the one who kept insisting that we stay together. I never would have expected you to stay behind."

"I know, I know," I replied. "I'm sorry. But if you'd seen the fear in that girl's face. I just couldn't let her be separated from her friend."

Mary said, "We waited and waited for another helicopter with you on it to land. A bunch of busses left. I insisted that we wait for you and the missing students. An official finally told me that no one else was getting out of Aguas Calientes today," she said. "I found Sara from the State Department among the people waiting for a bus. She explained that because of the rain, the last helicopters to depart flew directly to Cusco."

"So that's what happened," I exclaimed. "I think I was on the last helicopter out. It was raining pretty hard by then. When the pilot said he was going directly to Cusco, I worried that I wouldn't be able to get ahold of you. How did you manage to call Gustavus?"

"I used Sara's phone," Mary said with a laugh. "I didn't have your number, so I called CICE and told them to pass my message on to you."

"I was so relieved to get that call," I said.

"Yeah," Mary continued. "It was pretty funny. After I called and left the message for you, Sara asked me to call off our legislators. I asked what she meant. She said they'd been hammering their office in Lima with requests to get the Gustavus students out. Sara said the reason they moved to get us out today was because of the pressure they were getting from Minnesota legislators and the parents and friends of our students."

"Wow," I said. "We created quite a stir."

"There's been a lot in the press about Aguas Calientes, the threat of still more flooding, lack of food and water. Sara said there've been articles about growing tension among all the people trapped there; people sleeping on the streets, eating rice and beans provided by the Peruvian army. Parents were worried, so they called their legislators and pushed for action to get us out."

While it was great to get out when we did, it felt strange that it took the U.S. government to make it happen. The other stranded people were not as lucky. I could see how our departure must have looked to all the young people left at the gate. I wondered whether or not it had been a good move on the part of our government to get us out when they did.

The joy of having everyone back together proved stronger than my musings. I joined in the loud conversation. We all shared stories about our experiences on the helicopters and our transit back to Cusco. We toasted ourselves, the Peruvian army, Hector, Cris, Javier and the State Department. We ate and drank until everything was gone.

After dinner, exhausted and ready for bed, I headed to the lobby to check my messages. Carolyn sent me info about the flight we would take the following day at midnight from Lima. I walked back in and told the students, "The college is getting us tickets for tomorrow. The flight doesn't have a lot of openings, so they're still working on final booking." I continued, "You have tomorrow morning to explore Cusco. We'll leave for the airport about one p.m. and fly to Lima. Then Hector will give us a little tour of the capitol. We'll have our final group dinner, then head to the airport around ten p.m. for our flight home.

"We want to go out tonight to celebrate!" several students said.

"I don't know," I replied. "This is not the best place to be out late at night. You need to be careful."

Hector said, "If you go to places in the main plaza, you will be ok. But some people might try to sell you drugs."

"Great," I said, "that's just what I needed to hear."

"It's all right, Deb," said Julio said. "Some of us want to go out for a final celebration. We know how to be careful. Haven't we proved that? We can avoid the drug sellers. We'll be ok."

I was too tired to argue. "All right," I said, "but stay alert. Don't accept drinks from strangers."

"We know," Julio interrupted, adding by imitating my voice, "Stay together!"

13. Going Home

The next morning, I slept in and woke up slowly, stretching lazily. I felt relaxed and comfortable for the first time in several days. I gazed around the room and saw a huge hairy spider hanging on the wall at eye level next to the bed. I jumped up, grabbed one of my sandals and smacked it. The spider squished on the wall, leaving a gooey mess and a black spot from my sandal. It didn't wipe off. "Well, I guess I am leaving my mark in Peru," I chuckled to myself.

I joined Mary and several students for breakfast and checked my email. There was a message from Hector saying that he had our tickets to Lima. We didn't leave for the capitol until early afternoon, so everybody took time to wander the streets of Cusco. It was a sunny day, the air a little cool, and I loved that it wasn't raining.

I ducked into the cathedral to look at the beautiful altars and the Black Jesus statue. I'd heard during our earlier tour that the crucifix was black due the effect of centuries of candle smoke on the wood used to create it. Faithful locals called it the "Lord of the Earthquakes," believing the cross had stopped the tremors during a massive earthquake. Walking quietly through the cathedral, I felt the need to say a few prayers. I knelt down and breathed words of thanks for the Lord's help getting me through the past few days.

It happened to be Sarah H.'s birthday. I hunted down a bakery and bought a cake after explaining how to write "Happy Birthday, Sarah." The layer cake with fruit and cream filling was heavy. Back at the hotel, everyone gathered for lunch. We sang "Happy birthday" to Sarah H., who was twenty-two, and wished her well.

I asked the students, "So what did you do last night?"

"It was pretty laid back. A few of us went to a British Pub down the street and shared more stories from Aguas Calientes," said Brandon. "We also decided what we would eat first when we got back to the U.S."

"And what is that?" I asked.

I was surprised to learn that many of them wanted a salad with lots of stuff on it. Most of them also wanted a really big, juicy hamburger. While I was out, I stopped at an ATM for cash. Sarah H. got out the ledger and I paid off what I owed the students in Peruvian Soles, the only currency the ATM provided. I owed Mary Ellen so much I would have to repay her with dollars from the airport in Atlanta.

Then we said goodbye to Matt, who was heading back to his teaching position in Chile.

"Thanks for bailing me out," Matt said. "Without you guys, I don't know what I would have done for the last four days."

"No worries," I said. "You were a big help. Your Spanish is good, which made it easier to get around and figure things out when I needed help."

After lunch we headed to the Cusco airport. Flights between Cusco and Lima were also subject to the weather, so I was glad for sunshine. There would be no delays. When we were checking our bags, Javier and Cris surprised us by showing up. Everyone was happy to see them. We'd all wanted a chance to thank them. The two of them had left Aguas Calientes so suddenly that most of the students hadn't been able to say farewell. Javier said it had been a tough hike back to Cusco, even with other tour guides and local residents who were used to the terrain.

"What will you do now?" I asked, knowing that there wouldn't be any tourists heading to Machu Picchu for a long time.

"We're not sure," Javier answered. "This is our life, giving tours to Machu Picchu. Cris and I will just have to wait until we can work again."

Disturbed by this, Kevin pulled out the money I had just given back to him. He said quietly to the others, "Let's get a tip together for Javier and Cris, for all they did for us." Altogether, the students provided the equivalent of almost three hundred U.S. dollars for the two men.

"We can't take this," Javier protested.

"It's a tip for your extraordinary services," I replied. "The students want you to have it, to help you and your families until things get back to normal." Javier silently nodded his thanks and took the money.

Sarah H., who'd been the one to provide humor and lighthearted banter throughout the trip, also made sure everyone knew about her birthday. Javier and Chris brought her a small box of Peruvian candy, which she passed around. Finally, we had to head inside. It was hard. We hugged Javier and Cris one last time and thanked them again. What kind and gracious men those two were. I hoped I would see them again.

Our flight back to Lima was uneventful. The bright sun provided a beautiful view of the snow-capped Andes as we flew back to the capital. When we landed, Hector had a bus ready for a tour of the city. He told us the history of Lima as we wound through the narrow streets. We stopped at Plaza del Arma, the city's central square. We got out to walk around and have lunch before traveling back to Hostal Gémina, where we picked up the hand-made chairs Father Jack had given us. The chairs would have been too bulky to take to Machu Picchu, so we left them with the hotel owner. Mary and I planned to put them in our offices back at Gustavus, a nice remembrance.

That evening, Hector took us to a local restaurant for a farewell dinner. A bittersweet event, we were excited to be going home, but sorry that our adventure was coming to an end. We enjoyed one last Peruvian meal complete with tangy ceviche and pisco sours. We toasted Hector, and I tucked the rest of my Soles into his pocket to thank him. His presence had helped me so much, and I was grateful for his support and friendship.

Carolyn arranged for our tickets to be left at the airline desk. "I got tickets for everyone," she told me. "Three are first class. Seat assignments are randomly generated, but we want you and Mary to take two of the first-class seats. You're all on stand-by out of Atlanta. Hopefully, you'll get on that flight without difficulty."

"All right, First Class. Awesome!"

Standing in line to check our bags, I noticed a stand where oversized luggage could be wrapped in plastic to make it safer for travel. Mary and I figured that wrapping the folded chairs would make them easier to check as luggage. We handed over our credit cards and watched plastic sheets being wrapped and taped around each chair's bulky shape. After the chairs were encased like huge mummies, we hauled them over to the desk to drop them off.

"That will be two hundred dollars to ship the two chairs to the U.S.," said the agent.

"What? They're just another piece of luggage," I exclaimed. I wanted to take my chair home, but I didn't think the price was reasonable. The college had covered so many expenses to keep us safe and fed in Aguas Calientes, I was sure this would be one expense too many.

"No way," I said. "Mary," I asked, "do you want to pay to ship your chair home? I am going to pass."

"Not for one hundred dollars," she replied.

It was disappointing to have hauled the chairs all the way from Chimbote only to leave them at the Lima airport. I pulled out my phone, plugged it in next to the counter and called Hector. "Hector, I have a final gift for you, two hand-made folding chairs for your yard. They're under your name at the airport, Delta desk, all wrapped up and ready to go!"

"What?" he said. "The ones from Father Jack you stored at the hotel?"

"Yup. We can't afford to take them on the plane, so you can have them!"

"Oh, that will be nice." Hector said. "Thanks, Deb. I will get them tomorrow."

I hung up, feeling like I had made a good choice about the chairs, even though they would have looked nice in our offices. We picked up tickets and handed them out. Two students who had the first-class tickets hooted when they saw their seat assignment.

"Sorry gang," I said as I took back the two first class seats. "I'm going to pull rank. It would be unfair for only two of you to have first class accommodations, so Mary and I are going to take these seats. Thank you!" I smiled as I collected the tickets. By chance, Sarah H., our birthday girl, was assigned the other first-class ticket. The students laughed and told her that the ticket was her birthday gift from all of them. She smiled and waved her ticket in the air like a trophy.

We filed onto the plane, located our seats and got settled. The flight attendant checked her manifest then gave me a look. There was supposed to be a male sitting where I had parked myself.

"I am sorry, ma'am," she said. "You're in the wrong seat. You will need to go back to the economy section."

"No," I said. "I traded my ticket with one of my students. I'm keeping this seat."

"You can't do that," she replied. "You need to sit in the seat that was assigned to you."

"People switch seats all the time," I said. "It is no big deal."

"Not in first class," she responded. "I am afraid I must insist you move back to your assigned seat."

At this point, I'd had it. "I am not moving," I said, my voice rising. "I have had a horrific few days and I am keeping this first-class seat!" I clicked on my seatbelt, tightened it and glared at the attendant. She huffed and turned away. I felt a little guilty, but not too much. Mary grinned at me from her seat across the aisle and gave me a thumbs up. We both settled in for a relaxing flight home. I wanted to have a glass of wine and enjoy the luxuries of first-class, but I was so exhausted that my eyes began to close. I fell asleep before anything was served. As I nodded off, I noticed Sarah H. sitting across from us, enjoying every perk that was offered.

We had a layover in Atlanta that allowed for the students to treat themselves to their favorite American fast food. Although it was early morning, many of the students chowed down on burgers while Mary and I sipped coffee in the main food court. I hunted up another ATM machine and got enough cash to pay back Mary Ellen. The books were balanced. Finally, we could close the Bank of Deb.

When we arrived at the boarding gate, the ticket agent said there were more people on stand-by than there were available seats. "You'll need to wait until we check for no-shows," the attendant said.

"Ok," I replied. Again, we found ourselves sitting and waiting for information about how we would all get out. The students were nervous, concerned that not all of us would get on the plane together.

"What if there aren't enough seats?" Alyssa asked.

"Carolyn said she was trying to get us all out on the same flight," I replied, then repeated our mantra, "No one gets left behind, remember?"

I worried it might be upsetting for the students if they couldn't fly home together. They'd really bonded during our time in Peru. The students milled around munching snacks. We all wondered if someone might have to take a separate flight. It wouldn't be terrible. After all, we were back in the States, but the emotional reaction of the students concerned me. It would be difficult for anyone who didn't get on this flight.

When boarding began, our students all stood by anxiously waiting to hear their name called. As names were announced, I motioned for them to go ahead and board. I went up to the gate agent and said, "Excuse me. We're all from the same college, and it would be really great if we could all get on this flight. We were stranded in Peru for four days."

"I'm sorry," the gate attendant interrupted, "the flight is overbooked so it's highly likely that some people will not be able to get on this flight."

"That's not acceptable," I replied firmly. "These students need to depart together. All during our time in Peru, they supported each other and helped each other. You can't keep them here. Look at them," I implored, waving my hand to indicate the anxious faces of the students still waiting to hear their name.

She looked at me coolly and said, "I will call names in the order that I have them." On standby, the airline waits for those who have reservations. If people don't show up, they call up those on standby. A few of our students got tickets, then a few more. "Go on and board," I said to Mary and the students who'd been issued tickets. "I'll wait for the rest of us to get boarding passes."

A few minutes before we were scheduled to take off, everyone had tickets but Kevin. I looked around, and there was no one else waiting in the gate area. The agent was being officious and kept calling names for people who were obviously not there. Kevin looked up at me with big eyes and shrugged, acknowledging that he was not going anywhere. I went over and told him that if he didn't get a ticket, I would give him mine. I was adamant that all of the students land together in Minneapolis, so we waited.

Finally, I reached my limit. I went up to the gate agent and got in her face. "If you don't get this young man on this flight, the rest of the group is going to get off in protest. Then you'll have to find flights to re-book us all." I was normally not so intense, but recent days had increased my willingness to push for what I needed.

An attendant at the entrance to the jetway prepared to close the door.

The ticket agent paused, looked around the empty gate area, and finally called,

"Kevin Matuseski."

"As if there was anyone else waiting," I mumbled sarcastically. Kevin jumped up, got his ticket and hustled on board the plane, grinning. I followed quickly after uttering a hasty "Thank you" to the agent. I was last to board. Kevin, tall and gangly, made his way down the aisle, waving to his friends and high fiving them, the rest of the students cheered when he passed by on the way to his seat.

Flying home, I thought about how sweet it was that we were all finally heading back to our families. It would be great to see Jon. I'd be able to talk to my son without worrying about the phone not working or averting some new crisis. I thought it would be cool if the group could all exit the airport into the baggage claim area together. We were scattered throughout the plane, however, so that wouldn't happen. When we landed, the students grabbed their stuff, and hurried off the plane.

I waited to make sure all the students were off the plane, force of habit, I guess. I walked down to the international arrivals area. When I pushed through the door, it was like a circus. Parents and students were hugging and talking. Media people and cameras surrounded the baggage carousel as students pulled off bags. I smiled. It was great to hear the laughter and excitement. I spotted Jon, along with my sister MariBeth and brother-in-law, Reed. They were holding, 'Welcome home' balloons. I ran over and hugged Jon, getting a big welcome home kiss.

Mary and I were asked to talk to the reporters, and many of the students also gave brief statements. My sister told me to enjoy my fifteen minutes of fame as Mary and I relayed a bit about our experience.

"The main thing," I said to the reporters, "was that we were safe, and the students watched out for each other. We were in a better position than a lot of other people stranded there." I added, "I am proud of these young people. They managed the experience well, as would be expected of Gustavus students."

I waited to see all the students leave with their parents or head off to their rides, waving final goodbyes. After everyone from our group was gone, the silence and calm enveloped me. As we turned to go, Mary gave me a final hug. Smiling, she said, "When I signed on to accompany you on this trip, I didn't expect to have such a big adventure."

"You're right," I replied. "No one ever thought something like getting stranded by a flood would happen. It was so unexpected. But we made it through. Everyone is home safe." Waving, I watched as Mary walked off down the corridor. Jon put his arm around me, and I hugged him again. I felt so relieved, and so very tired. I also felt a huge sense of accomplishment. I smiled, and as we headed out of the airport, I looked around one more time, making sure no one was left behind.

24. Sunset at the mission in Chimbote.

Afterward

A t times, when I think back on my experience in Peru, it feels like it happened to someone else. I have strong memories from the event, but they seem distant, maybe because I had to jump back into the real world upon our return. The college needed me to help make sense of the expenses for the Peru trip. I spent a day going over the few receipts I had, explaining how I used the money I'd gotten from the ATM's.

There were no recriminations, just a need to clarify. I had receipts up until the first day we were stranded. After that, things got so hectic that I rarely remembered to ask for a receipt. Many of the smaller places where we ate did not offer receipts. When I explained things like leaving money for the hotel owner to reserve our rooms, the budget director said, "We'll just call that a tip."

We labeled a lot of things "tips," "donations," or "supplies" when I had no documentation for the expenditure. Even with my poor accounting, the college managed to balance the budget for the course. Insurance helped with the additional flight expenses, as well as covering unexpected costs for the days we were stranded in Peru. I was grateful for the positive response from my colleagues and administrators.

Newspaper articles told stories of our adventure. I received a few requests to speak about the experience. Students shared stories and memories at a poignant Chapel Talk on campus later in the spring of 2010. Not unexpectedly, the students kept in close contact. They often held *Peru Days* to meet up for dinner and beverages, and to reconnect.

I keep one newspaper article about the event tacked on the bulletin board in my office, a piece from my hometown paper, the Mason City *Globe Gazette*. I smile whenever I reread the comments my mom gave to a reporter after I returned from Peru.

MASON CITY, February 3, 2010: Debra Pitton is a college professor and world traveler.

The Newman High School graduate's most recent trip, to the ancient Inca ruins of Machu Picchu in the Andes Mountains of Peru sounds positively Indiana Jones-like. Pitton, an education professor at Gustavus Adolphus College in St. Peter, Minnesota., another professor, and 21 Gustavus students were airlifted from the Machu Picchu area last week after local railroad tracks were destroyed by flooding. ...

"She loves adventure," said Pitton's mother, Beth Eckerman of Mason City, "but I thought maybe this was one adventure too much." ... Eckerman said her daughter, who also has guided students on trips to London, Costa Rica and Spain, is energetic, and "can handle about any situation. ... She did a lot of Girl Scouting in her youth, and I think she used all her Girl Scout tricks to keep everybody happy on the trip, keeping everybody calm, keeping everybody together and safe," Eckerman said.

Mason City Globe Gazette ©2010

Leave it to my mom to ignore any of my advanced learning. She chalked up our survival in Peru to Girl Scout training. It was humbling. And she was right, adventure was a part of scouting and a strong enticement for me to take on the course. My mom's characterization of the trip as being, "one adventure too much," was also true, in fact, it was really so much more than I could have ever anticipated.

The response from people, when hearing about our situation, often surprised me. I was once talking to a group about the evacuation when someone asked, "Who was paying for the helicopters and stuff?"

"It was a joint effort." I responded. "The U.S. paid the fuel costs for the Peruvian helicopters. They did this to help Americans and everyone else get out. The evacuation used both Peruvian army helicopters as well as U.S. choppers."

"Did any other country come to help their people get out?" came another question.

"No," I replied. Some in the group nodded in agreement to my answer, saying that the U.S. had been a hero in this situation. I continued, "I'm not sure the U.S. can take all the glory. It was the Peruvian Army who really took charge. I've read that other South American governments wanted to send in helicopters. The leaders in Peru, however, managed the evacuation, aided by the U.S. Embassy."

At the time, it made perfect sense for Sara and J.J. to get the Peruvian army to help us leave first. But it had felt incredibly uncomfortable walking out ahead of so many who were still stranded. I was sure that local residents were going to be the last out, if they were evacuated at all. Thinking back on it now, I'm still conflicted, I wonder whether we should have been taken out before others.

After our return, I tried to follow the news from Peru, curious to know what had happened to the people of Aguas Calientes. I found some interesting information on the internet.

One post on the *Associated Press* website dated January 26 read: "A mudslide on the famed Inca trail to Machu Picchu in Peru killed an Argentine tourist and a Peruvian guide Tuesday, as authorities evacuated dozens of tourists by helicopter."

A series of Tweets posted by the Latin American News, @lanewsupdate, a media monitor/analyst covering Latin America, provided eye-opening information.

> *2010-01-26   7:59pm*—*Routes opened, connections between Cusco and Ollantaytambo: Road clearances and use of alternate routes when available, means land routes are now open from Ollantaytambo to Cusco, allowing supplies to get into the sacred valley and people to get out. There are as many as 2000 trapped in Aguas Calientes, still inaccessible by its single train connection. Ferried out by helicopters, their rescue may take days.*
>
> *2010-01-27 8:51pm*—*United States Apologies: The US embassy in Peru has apologized for sending helicopters to the flood region to rescue only US citizens and not help others in need based on health or age. "We shouldn't have done that," they say, after having evacuated all US nationals.*
>
> *2010-01-28 12:01pm*—*Still up to 1000 tourists trapped in Aguas Calientes: Authorities report those stranded in Aguas Calientes now number around 1000. Tourists there*

complain of a lack of food and water, and Peruvian
authorities admit as much but state that they are safe for now.
2010-01-29, 7:05pm— *All Tourists Rescued:*
Authorities have announced that all tourists have now be
evacuated from Aguas Calientes, with further checks for
stragglers to take place tomorrow.

The post about the American Embassy's apology floored me. I
didn't hesitate when Sara and J.J. told us their plan. I thought they
knew best. My ignorance of international relations and blind faith
in our State Department put all of us into a potentially dangerous
situation. My concern about leaving before others was validated.
The fact that people died confirmed the danger we felt was real.

The Website, *LivinginPeru.com* published an article by Nathan
Paluck on January 27. He provided a compilation of the news
stories. Special correspondent Andre Dare reported the following:

Martín Pérez, Minister of Foreign Trade and Tourism,
expects that 800 to 1,000 stranded tourists will be airlifted
today, Jan. 28, from Machu Picchu town, "provided the
weather allows it. If weather conditions are good, we might
start as early as 7 a.m. so we could have another 3 or 4 hours
and carry 300 or 400 more people," he added. In addition,
according to some Peruvian passengers rescued from Machu
Picchu town, some public health workers based there have
allegedly issued fake health certificates to certain tourists, after
being paid in cash, in order to allow them priority in the
evacuation flights. Minister Perez remarked that no one has
to pay to be airlifted, and that there is no discrimination
regarding the distribution of official help.

Reading about the bribery was shocking. People had paid for
paperwork to allow them out earlier! This had created a tense
situation for those of us who tried to follow the rules.

The timeline for recovery was quicker than I expected. An article
in the *Economist* on February 11, 2010 entitled "Making do without
Machu Picchu," stated: "The government issued a decree for the
rapid rebuilding of the railway, which is operated by PeruRail, an
affiliate of Orient-Express Hotels, a Bermuda-based company."

The daily loss of tourism income was no doubt a concern. I was
glad that rebuilding happened at a rapid pace. On March 13, 2010,

News.com.au posted: "A senior official announced Peru's main tourist attraction Machu Picchu, one of the world's most prized heritage sites, will re-open on March 29 after heavy rains cut off the ancient citadel earlier this year."

All of this information made me stop and reflect. The situation had been dangerous. People died due to the flood and mudslides. Getting out safely was a big concern. Still, if I had known that people were offering money to the officials to leave first, would I have done it? I was focused on getting us home, trying every means possible to finagle a way out. I hadn't been above tipping (bribing) the hotel clerk to keep our rooms. But if I could have bribed the people at the gate, would I have done it? I don't know how the students would have reacted if I'd tried that route. Some would definitely not have been ok with such a plan. I wasn't sure I would have been ok with such a plan. Luckily, I hadn't thought of bribery as an option, so I was spared that moral dilemma.

What had the people of Aguas Calientes done after the flood? I asked this question of tour guide David Villagra, who I connected with on-line. He had been there during the whole situation and described the local response. "Some people went to Cusco to find work, but most stayed. People did not want to leave their homes and businesses. Families formed groups to cook and eat together," he said. "The government and wealthy owners of the big hotels kept supplies coming in on helicopters. It was not a lot, but people were able to be in their homes. Staying in the village kept the government aware of the ongoing needs of the people. The citizens of Machu Picchu did not want the government to forget their situation."

I was glad PeruRail and gotten service to Machu Picchu going again so quickly. Having viewed the devastation, it really was amazing. When I returned to the village in 2012, I noticed that while most services were up and running, the streets of the town were still torn up from the flood. It took several more years to return the community to the way it was before the disaster.

I also wondered how the experience affected my students. Reading their final reflection papers, it seemed every day had provided new insights for the Gusties. The course impacted people in different ways, but their reflections spoke of their expanded awareness and perspective.

One paper that particularly touched me was from Kyle J. He said, he was "mad at me." After experiencing poverty and the daily life of many Peruvians, he couldn't go back to the way he thought about the poor before going to Peru. He wanted to return to his old way of thinking—but he couldn't. He said he was wrestling with these perspectives, trying to incorporate them into a new way of seeing the world. For another course, Kyle organized a drive to collect children's books to be sent to Peru as an addition to the English library we started.

Many students' reflections focused on their work in Chimbote and the kindness of the local people. Nursing students spoke sadly about the illness and sickness they witnessed, and the lack of medical support for the poor. They had struggled with the unsanitary conditions. The fact that people suffered from diseases and injuries that were easily managed in the U.S., troubled them.

While the students included comments about our plight in Machu Picchu, it was not the main point of their reflections. I was gratifyed to read about their new awareness of the perspectives of others. Their writing included strong insights regarding the impact of culture and poverty, and of their own privilege.

I was glad to note that students identified the positive impact of working and living alongside the Peruvians in Chimbote. Katie, an elementary education major, wrote that the course, "opened my eyes to how closely connected education is to the process of alleviating poverty. Prior to this experience, the view I had of helping the poor was giving them food, water and shelter. Now I know that education is the key to ending poverty."

Sarah H. also spoke of a change in her thinking. "I was consumed by my effect on the poor, being the one helping the needy. But they helped me. The people of Chimbote taught me about the value and importance of community—of solving problems together."

I have traveled to Chimbote, Peru, three more times since that first course in January 2010, providing a total of seventy-nine Gustavus students an opportunity to share the Peruvian experience. These students provided service to the Chimbote community and explored the Peruvian culture at Machu Picchu. My goal was to design an opportunity for learning beyond the walls of the college. I wanted to create an experience that would hopefully shift the thinking of young people by immersing them in another culture through service. Most students' final reflections echoed the comments and learning experiences of the first group related to their work with the people of Chimbote.

Though none of these later experiences were as adventure-filled as the 2010 visit, each had to deal with its own particular situations. One time we all caught the flu and had to manage our illness with only one bathroom. Another year we had to wait out a wildfire ranging across the desert on our way back to Lima by bus.

While writing this book, I reached out to the students who traveled with me that initial year. I asked for any thoughts or insights, particularly related to the time we were stranded. Seven years had passed, and unfortunately, I was not able to reconnect with everyone. The students I did meet with or hear from corroborated my memories and added their own perspectives.

Julio said that in Peru he found a place where he looked and sounded like everyone else. Although he was not exactly like the Peruvians, he fit in there in a way that he sometimes did not in the States. His ability to translate and provide support throughout our time in Peru gave him a unique status and a perspective different from the rest of us.

"Because I could navigate all that was happening so easily in both Chimbote and Aguas Calientes," said Julio, "I felt my American privilege very strongly. I knew that because I had my little blue book, my U.S. passport, I would go home eventually. Even if I was like the Peruvians, I had something they didn't have." He added, "I struggled with the animosity toward us when State Department officials walking us out to the helicopters. I felt bad for those still waiting to leave, but happy to be getting out. I still wonder about that. Was it right for us to leave then? Still, all-in-all, it was a grand adventure!"

Mary and I also reminisced about the experience as I prepared to write this book. She said, "I had very mixed feelings about the whole drama of our departure from Aguas Calientes. Not least of all was my renewed awareness of the privilege we, as U.S. citizens, so often assume. We somehow feel entitled to go to the head of the line in situations where everyone is anxious, frightened and nearing desperation."

Kevin, writing about our departure from Machu Picchu for a graduate course, said, "I was very nervous. When I saw the crowd we were going to have to walk through I thought it was going to be very uncomfortable. And it was. The whole situation raises a lot of questions for me. Because the U.S. was funding the fuel for the helicopters, did we as U.S. citizens have the right to be evacuated first? Even if nationality is valued, does it even matter where we are from if we are eventually thrown into one melting pot abroad? Should we retain the privilege that comes with our birthplace even when we are no longer in our place of birth?"

Kevin's comments mirrored my thinking about the experience in Aguas Calientes. It was only after I was home that I was able to think clearly about the events and our behavior in Peru. I realize that putting the course together, pulling it off and getting the students home safely, provided me with a huge opportunity for self-awareness. I think more about the privileges I have as an American citizen, especially when I am traveling abroad. I recognize how Americans are perceived by other countries, and that it is not always favorable. I feel a responsibility to help shape a more positive relationship between U.S. travelers and the local members of the communities we visit.

I have been asked why I go back to Peru after what some would consider a harrowing experience in 2010.

"Didn't you worry that something like the flood could happen again?" I am often asked.

I always reply, "I go back because the work students do in Peru is a powerful learning experience. It makes a difference in the lives of the college students who participate."

How did this experience influence the 2010 students? Many former Peru travelers, now graduated, are involved in service work. Besides teaching and health care, these young people are involved in careers that expand their global perspectives. Julio now works for the ACLU, supporting Latino services in southern Minnesota. Molly, who taught for a year in South America, takes her Minneapolis high school students on service-learning trips to South America every other year. Jennifer got a job as a nurse at a hospital in New York and signed on to return to Chimbote in 2011 with a medical mission team.

Jenna and Sarah H. volunteered at a fundraising dinner for the Chimbote mission. Kevin spent the first few years of his career teaching in Columbia before returning to teach in the Twin Cities. Kyle G. works with the College Advising Corps, a national nonprofit that supports college access for all. Chelsey Kr spent a year teaching in Palestine.

A letter from Kyle J. exemplifies the impact of the course and reflects my hope for all students who travel and study abroad:

> *Working in health care, I have seen patients and families that are battling poverty, and I believe that I am better equipped to understand what sort of problems they face in their life—problems that I have been fortunate not to have experienced. It is easy to grow frustrated with patients in poverty. Often, they are non-compliant with treatment plans (due to lack of money or resources) which can be a source of irritation to the physician—leading to lack of empathy towards the patient.*

> *Given my experience in Peru—seeing poverty up close and how it creates many obstacles to completing "simple" tasks for most, I have gained insight that will ideally insulate me from growing frustrated and dismissive with patients dealing with poverty. I hope to use my experience visiting Chimbote, Peru, to be a more compassionate physician to my patients.*

Education, Healthcare and Poverty in Peru, 2010

Student name	Major
Nicole Abel	nursing
Sara Bentley	nursing
Elise Biewen	art education
Joshua Busacker	psychology
Alyssa Fitzgerald	social studies/history/education
Brita Gilyard	nursing
Kyle Goodfellow	psychology
Brandon Hirdler	political science/history
Sarah Hoerr	public accounting
Laura Jensen	nursing and Spanish
Kyle Johnson	biology
Katie Kaderlik	elementary education
Chelsey Kollodge-Hayes	elementary education
Chelsey Krusemark	com arts/literature/teaching
Molly Koppel	com arts/literature/teaching
Mary Ellen Korby	elementary education
Kevin Matuseski	com arts/literature/teaching
Alison Oppenheimr	com arts/literature/teaching
Jeanifer Poon	nursing
Jenna Rusnacko	communication studies
Julio Zelaya	political science

Acknowledgements

I want to thank the Gustavus students and my colleague, Mary Solberg, who traveled with me to Peru in 2010. I appreciate their support during the events of this story, and I am glad they were along for the adventure. Several of the students provided additional insights and read early editions of the book, ensuring that the events were accurate. I want to thank my family and friends who encouraged me to put this story down on paper and for reading early editions. Thanks also go to Loretta Ellsworth, a friend and author who steered me in the right direction when I began to write, and to Tom Driscoll, managing editor of Shipwreckt Books, who helped shape my story.

Photo Index

Endnote

/*i* *Three Cups of Tea,* *(*Penguin, 2007*)* by Greg Mortenson and David Oliver Relin, recounts Greg Mortenson's story of becoming lost on K2, wandering into a Pakistani village and being welcomed. When he learns that there is no school for girls, he raises funds, starts and heads the non-profit Central Asia Institute (CAI), and oversees the construction of 171 schools. CAI reported that these schools provide education to over 64,000 children, including 54,000 girls.

Three Cups of Tea was on the New York *Times* bestseller list from 2007 to 2010.

I led the trip of twenty-one Gustavus Adolphus students to Peru, and recommended we all read *Three Cups of Tea,* in January 2010.

In April of 2011, CBS *60 Minutes* correspondent Steve Kroft described inaccuracies in Mortenson's book *Three Cups of Tea* and its sequel, *Stones into Schools: Promoting Peace with Books, Not Bombs, in Afghanistan and Pakistan,* as well as financial improprieties in the operation of the Central Asia Institute. In particular, CBS News disputed Mortenson's claim that he got lost near K2 and ended up in Korphe, his capture by the Taliban in 1996, the number of schools built and supported by CAI, and the propriety of using CAI funds for Mortenson's book tours.

60 Minutes made the following allegations:

—The events recounted in *Three Cups of Tea*: Mortenson getting lost on the way down from K2, stumbling into Korphe, and promising to build a school, did not take place.

—The story recounted in *Stones into Schools* about Mortenson's capture by the Taliban did not occur. His purported kidnappers state he was a guest, and the Taliban did not exist in the country at that time.

—Schools that the Central Asia Institute claims to have built either have not been built, have been built and abandoned, are used for other purposes such as grain storage, or have not been supported by CAI after they were built.

—The amount of money Central Asia Institute spends on advertising Mortenson's books and paying the travel expenses of his speaking tours, including hiring private jets, is excessive relative to other comparable charitable institutions.

About the Author

D ebra Eckerman Pitton was born and raised in Mason City, Iowa. A backpacking trip to California in high school and a European choir tour with Loras College sparked her interest in travel. After teaching in middle school and high school, she completed her Ph.D. and joined the Education Department at Gustavus Adolphus College in St. Peter, Minnesota. Debra has written and published numerous academic texts and articles related to teaching and mentoring. An advocate for both global and service learning, she combined these interests to develop and teach international travel classes. During the international courses, students teach English or work to support local communities. Debra currently lives in Burnsville, Minnesota, with her husband Jon. They have three married children and a wonderful granddaughter. The entire family enjoys traveling and exploring new places.

25. Deb Pitton, Machu Picchu, 2010.